The Symposium

and

The Phaedo

Crofts Classics

GENERAL EDITOR

Samuel H. Beer, *Harvard University*

PLATO

The Symposium
and
The Phaedo

TRANSLATED AND EDITED BY

Raymond Larson

SAINT JOHN'S UNIVERSITY
COLLEGEVILLE, MINNESOTA

HARLAN DAVIDSON, INC.
Wheeling, Illinois 60090-6000

Visit us on the World Wide Web at www.harlandavidson.com.

Library of Congress Catalog Card Number
79-55731
ISBN 0-88295-119-X
ISBN 978-0-88295-122-5
ISBN 0-88295-122-X

Manufactured in the United States of America
07 06 05 9 10 11 CM

contents

introduction

The *Symposium* and the *Phaedo* are two of Plato's most
delightful and interesting dialogues, dealing, respectively,
with the nature of *eros* (love or sexual attraction) and the
immortality of the soul. They differ sharply in setting and
mood. The *Symposium* recounts a party held at the home of a
fashionable poet who is entertaining some well-known
celebrities. The *Phaedo* presents a discussion held in a prison
cell, where Socrates is spending his last day with some
humble companions. The guests at the party play a kind of
intellectual parlor game in which they show off their
brilliance by making speeches on love. The companions
in prison discuss immortality, a topic appropriate to the
occasion: Socrates' imminent death. The rowdy *Symposium*
ends in a revel and sleep; the elegiac *Phaedo* closes with
Socrates' death. In neither dialogue does Socrates succumb to
the mood, and he remains calm and unaffected throughout
both.

the forms

Both dialogues presuppose an acquaintance with those
peculiar Platonic entities, the forms. The forms arose
something like this: As we look around us, the world presents
to our senses a confused heap of ceaselessly changing
particular things and an incessant bombardment of
particular, random events. Particular things and events are
all that we ever perceive. Each particular thing is unique,
distinct from every other. No two roses are exactly alike; no
snowflake precisely resembles another. Yet we instantly
recognize all roses as roses and all snowflakes as snowflakes.
How do we do it? Not with our senses. They only give us
impressions of particular things; they do not sort them out.

The world would be a wild and terrible place if our minds did not somehow apprehend relations that allow us to divide the jumble of perceived things into classes and the swarm of events into ordered progressions. These relations I shall call "universals." Each universal gives its name ("rose," "snowflake," "equality," "beauty," etc.) to every particular thing that belongs to its class. Our ability to grasp universals is what enables us to recognize and name roses and snowflakes and everything else. It also enables us to think and to speak, and to acquire such understanding of the world as we have. The mind, which floundered helplessly in a sea of particulars as long as it had only the senses to observe with, now has something firm to hold on to. In this respect, universals are more solid and stable than particulars.

The ability to recognize universals, to see relations and form conceptions, is absolutely essential to human existence, even on the most primitive level. Without it, the world would be incomprehensible. There could be no thought, speech, or knowledge; and man would have to live solely by instinct and habit, like an animal, with no possibility of ever changing his condition.

But the situation is a paradoxical one because these universals, so essential to thought and so solid and stable to the mind, have no solid, physical existence. They are bodiless, invisible and intangible. Take any physical objects—two wooden rulers, for instance. Looking at them we may say: "I see two rulers." But this statement is not literally true: We see the rulers, but not the "two." Again, we may say "I see equal rulers," and again the statement goes beyond what we actually see: We see only the rulers, not the equality. The rulers are there on the table, but where are the universals, the "two" and the "equal"? We have to admit that wherever they are, they are not in the physical world. From this observation we may draw a general conclusion: Particular things exist, or seem to exist, in the world that we perceive with our senses (the "sensible" world); universals exist in a world that we apprehend with intelligence (the "intelligible" world).

We also know that our rulers are not really equal, even though we agree to regard them as such. Even if they could be perfectly machined, they would still differ in length at the atomic level. Equality, however, never falls short of perfection. We thus arrive at our second conclusion:

Particulars are always imperfect; universals are perfect.

Finally, we may look at our two rulers and try to imagine what they were in the past and what they will become in the future. A few years ago they were parts of living trees (it would be hard to say what they were before that). Now they are dead artifacts. A thousand years from now they probably will not exist at all, at least not in a form that we could easily recognize. They are in a continual process of change. In fact, they are changing before our very eyes, as we could see if we had a sufficiently powerful microscope. Heraclitus, a pre-Socratic philosopher, summed up this process in a famous saying: "Everything flows." In Plato's words, things like our rulers are always "becoming," or "coming into being and passing away." Ceaseless change, therefore, characterizes everything in the sensible world, from electrons to galaxies. But what about things in the intelligible world, like twoness and equality? What were *they* a hundred (or a million) years ago, and what will *they* become in the future? The answer is obvious: Time and change do not affect them; they do not "flow." In Plato's words they do not "become;" they always *"are."* Thus we reach our third conclusion: Particular things are transitory and always changing; universals are eternal and unchanging.

We may sum up our conclusions by saying that particulars are perceptible, imperfect, and changing; universals are imperceptible, perfect, and unchanging. The two classes, the sensible and the intelligible, therefore have opposite characteristics. Is there any relation between them? There doesn't seem to be much. We know universals, but we cannot see them; we see particulars, but we cannot know them. I can know (in the sense of define and intellectually apprehend) "catness," or *cat* in the abstract, but I cannot in that sense "know" the cat purring in my lap. The more I look at him, in fact, the more evanescent he becomes, like the Chesire Cat, who keeps vanishing and reappearing until Alice exclaims: "You make one quite giddy!" I too am caught in a giddy predicament because if the sensible and the intelligible realms are unconnected, if what I see has nothing to do with what I know, then there is no necessary connection between my thought and the external world, between "knowledge" and "reality." The mind recoils from this impasse and tries to find a way out, a bridge that will join the two realms.

Plato discovered a whole system of bridges and christened them "forms." The forms *are* the intelligible world, and they not only connect the sensible and the intelligible realms, but they actually cause the world of sense. Now, when we contemplate the chaos presented to us by our senses and then compare that with the relative order revealed to our minds through universals, we are (or ought to be) struck dumb with wonder. There must be some powerful force at work here. It seems like magic. And that, according to Plato, is just about what is is. The forms are universals—timeless, invariable, and perfect—which enjoy true existence outside the world of sense. They are not ideas that exist in our minds, but objective realities that would exist even if there were no minds to perceive them. (Therefore the traditional translation of forms as "ideas" is misleading in modern English.) From some vital force that causes them to throw shadows or reflections, the forms give rise to the motley collection of darting, shifting, fleeting particulars that make up our world, lending them a sort of shadow existence. The forms therefore cause the particulars, to which they stand in the relation of originals to copies. Our world of transient, changing particulars is merely a pale reflection or a wavering copy of the eternal, unchanging world of forms. There are innumerable forms, one for every conceivable universal, and particular things "participate" in them in various complicated and shifting ways to produce this pageant that our senses perceive. We can have knowledge only of these intelligible forms, and only our souls can grasp them. Of perceptible things we cannot have knowledge, but only a sort of quasi knowledge, which Socrates calls "opinion."

Socrates refers to the forms in various ways. Besides "forms," he also calls them "shapes" and "figures." More often, he uses expressions on the pattern of "the beautiful (or the equal, etc.) itself" or "the beautiful that *is*," where the italicized *is* denotes "true existence."

dialectic and myth

The *Symposium* and the *Phaedo* present two important ways of dealing with forms. One is dialectic, Socrates' method of question and answer, which aims at truth. The *Symposium* sets dialectic against rhetoric, which aims at persuasion. Using dialectic, Socrates reveals the truth about Love and thus defeats the other speakers, whose rhetoric merely reveals conflicting opinions. In the *Phaedo* Socrates contrasts dialectic with observation, the method of the natural sciences. Observation uncovers facts, but not the truth that governs the facts. Both dialogues show that only dialectic can lead the mind from opinion and deceptive appearance to truth.

The other way, closely connected with dialectic, is myth. The whole *Symposium* is cast in the form of a myth, and the *Phaedo* culminates in a myth. The importance of myth is this: Dialectic, an activity of the reasoning faculty, has mainly a negative function. It forces us to recognize the discrepancy (mentioned in the Section above) between thought and perception, and it convinces us of the need for clearing up this discrepancy. But reason alone cannot clear it up; that is a task for our intuitive or imaginative faculty. We must "see" the forms directly in a revelation. But before that can happen, two things are required: Our reason must be made aware of the discrepancy and convinced of the need for clearing it up, and our soul's intuitive faculty must be awakened and prepared for the revelation. The first is the task of dialectic, the second of myth. One purpose of myth, then, is to exercise our intuition and make it receptive to revelation. Another purpose of myth is to express the revelation once it has been seen. Ordinary language cannot adequately express suprarational truth; that requires special modes of expression, such as metaphor, simile, and myth—the language of mystics and poets. Myth is therefore both a preparation for and an expression of the revelation of the forms. Once the forms have been revealed, however, thought can contemplate them directly. This direct contemplation of the forms is again dialectic. Dialectic, therefore, is both the rational process of arriving at specific truths by question and answer and the intellectual contemplation of ultimate truth after it has been revealed to a soul made receptive by myth.

greek homosexuality

A modern reader, bemused by the sexual attitudes that Plato's characters seem to display, may shake his head in wonder and say of the Greeks what Herodotus says of the Egyptians: "They reverse the manners and customs of the rest of mankind." This observation holds true for the Athenian leisure class, the circle in which Socrates habitually moved. When a Greek of the classical period speaks of love, he is normally thinking of homosexual love. The Greeks envisioned the ideal love relationship as one between a young man (the "lover") and a teenage boy (the "loved one"). Both parties had to follow rigid rules and conventions to escape public disapproval. Custom demanded that the lover "pursue," the loved one "flee." The lover was expected to court his loved one, to shower him with gifts and attention, to dote on him, and to serve him like a slave. The loved one, on the other hand, was supposed to be modest, passive, and hard to get. With perseverance and luck, a worthy lover might finally attain the ultimate bliss of sexual union with his loved one. A pretty boy could expect to begin his sexual career as an ardently pursued loved one. Later, when mature, he would assume the active role of lover, eagerly pursuing other young beauties. Such love was considered admirable, even ennobling. Heterosexual love was held to be rather vulgar; a man married to have children, but he directed his erotic impulses toward young men. Unfortunately, we know very little about the love lives of Greek women. The lower classes were much more heterosexual, but even among them homosexual affairs were common.

The Greek custom resembles medieval courtly love, except that the boy replaces the high-born, married lady as the object of desire. Both conventions were artificial and stylized, both enjoined strict rules of etiquette, and although their ideals were often betrayed in practice, both conventions inspired men to transcend their selfish, earthbound interests and aspire to a higher goal. To what heights the practice of "proper boy love" could lead may be seen in Plato's *Symposium.*

the symposium

A symposium was a drinking party. Normally, it seems to have been an intimate affair with only a few guests, invited first for dinner. Like all things Greek, a symposium was a formal activity, with a "master of ceremonies" and rules for everything from the seating arrangement to the drinking procedure. The guests might play games, sing drinking songs, or be amused by professional entertainers (jesters, flute girls, etc.) such as appear in Xenophon's *Symposium.*[1]

[1] **Translated** by the present author in *The Apology and Crito of Plato and the Apology and Symposium of Xenophon,* (Lawrence, Kansas: Coronado Press, 1980).

Conversation was also important. A topic would be set for the guests to discuss (as in Xenophon) or to give speeches on (as in Plato). The drinking might be moderate, as in Xenophon, or heavy. In Plato's *Symposium* the guests agree at the beginning "to drink more for pleasure than to get drunk" (176e). Like other good intentions, this one is soon forgotten, and the symposium degenerates into a revel.

In form, the *Symposium* and the *Phaedo* are both indirect dialogues. A character in the direct dialogue tells a story to a group of friends, and this narrated story constitutes the main dialogue. The *Phaedo* is thus a tale within a tale. But the *Symposium* is a tale within a tale within a tale, and at its climax it contains yet another tale within these three. It may therefore seem confusing unless one understands the situation.

The narrator of the *Symposium* is Apollodorus, an enthusiastic follower of Socrates who also appears in the *Phaedo*. The *Symposium* plunges us into the middle of a conversation that Apollodorus is having with some unnamed companions. They have obviously just asked him to tell them about a party given by the tragic poet Agathon. The dialogue does not open with the question, but with Apollodorus's reply: he answers indirectly by repeating a similar request made of him "the day before yesterday." Everything moves by indirection; the reader must infer the present request from the request of two days earlier. This brief reported conversation establishes several facts: The symposium took place long ago; it was held to celebrate the victory of Agathon's first tragedy (in 416 B.C.), when these characters (and Plato as well) were still only children. Apollodorus, therefore, could not have been present. He got the story from a man named Aristodemus, who had been there. We learn that Agathon moved out of Athens "years ago," but he is spoken of as being still alive. From other sources we know that Agathon left Athens about 407 B.C. and died around 401; therefore the external dialogue must take place about 402 B.C. The main dialogue, then, will be Apollodorus's version of Aristodemus's account of a party held some fourteen years earlier.

Apollodorus is characterized in the opening scene of the *Symposium* as a sharp-tongued fanatic (his nickname is "Maniac") who is impatient with his friends for not sharing his fanaticism for philosophy. The *Phaedo* presents him as having little control over his emotions, and Xenophon calls him "rather simple" (*Apology* 28). Aristodemus also is characterized in the *Symposium* as a simple soul (Socrates implies as much before they leave for the party), a barefoot enthusiast who, we learn later, was a poor drinker, became drowsy, and even fell asleep before the party was over. Plato seems to have gone out of his way to find unreliable informants to narrate his dialogue.

The guests at Agathon's symposium had given speeches in praise of Love. Apollodorus narrates these speeches as he heard them from Aristodemus, using the formula: "He (Aristodemus) said that he (the speaker) said." When we come to the climactic speech of Socrates, however, we reach an even deeper level of reported speech. Socrates does not give a speech of his own but purports to repeat an account that he allegedly heard from a mysterious lady named Diotima (whom he has probably just invented). At the climax of the *Symposium*, therefore, we actually have five levels of reported speech: Plato is presenting Apollodorus's version of Aristodemus's account of Socrates' speech about Diotima's explanation of Love. Several times Plato stresses the faulty memories of the speakers as they narrate events that took place many years before: "Aristodemus couldn't remember every speech in detail, and I can't remember everything he told me." (178a).

The *Symposium*'s complicated structure reflects Plato's view of reality: Our world of sense is merely a faint, distorted echo of the intelligible world (of forms) which exists forever unchanged beyond this world of change and illusion. The narration of this dialogue resembles the party game in which each person passes on a saying that has been whispered in his ear; by the end of the line the saying has usually been distorted almost beyond recognition. In the same way, Diotima's true explanation of Love reaches us only through a series of reports, each distorted by faulty memory and the passage of time.[2]

The Love speeches in the *Symposium* are closely linked

---

[2] **The point** is made later, more subtly, that memory is by nature deceptive. In Socrates' speech (208a), Diotima says that "reviewing preserves knowledge by implanting a fresh, seemingly identical memory to replace a departing one." The new memory only *seems* identical with the earlier one. The word here translated as "reviewing" has the same stem as the word Apollodorus uses in the

and form an ascending progression from the particular to the universal, from the selfish to the selfless, from the mundane to the sublime. Each speaker builds on the previous speeches, amplifying and correcting what has already been said.

Phaedrus, the first speaker, opens on a crass, utilitarian note by praising Love as useful to society. Love is a great god who inspires lovers with a sense of shame that makes them behave decently in public and who promotes a spirit of self-sacrifice that makes loved ones willing to die for their lovers. Phaedrus presents love as self-centered and sterile, a force that leads ultimately to death; his final word is "dead."

Pausanias, the second speaker, argues more subtly, but also more perversely. He begins by distinguishing between physical ("common") and spiritual ("heavenly") Love and then goes on ostensibly to praise spiritual Love but in reality to justify sexual intercourse between love partners. He bases his argument on moral relativity: Acts in themselves are morally neutral; their goodness or badness depends on how they are performed. Sexual gratification is good if performed for the sake of self-improvement. The goal of love is therefore sex for self-improvement: selfish means to a selfish end. Pausanias's subtlety masks a cruel and banal egotism, echoed by the brutal harshness of his style.

After a bit of comic by-play involving Aristophanes' hiccups, Eryximachus the doctor speaks. His style is as smooth and flowing as Pausanias's was harsh and abrupt, and he characterizes himself as the opposite of Pausanias: soft, effeminate, and prissy. His argument is pedantic and confused, a parody of scholarly double-talk. His main contribution is to lift Love out of the constricted sphere of human affairs and present him as a universal, cosmic force that rules all of nature.

Aristophanes the comedian speaks next, in the style familiar to us from his comedies—at once sobor and fantastic, earthy and elegant. His exuberant imagination creates a zany myth about primordial men who were spherical in shape and divided into three sexes instead of only two. As always with

opening sentence, translated there as "practiced." By "practicing" or "reviewing" the story of the symposium a couple of days before this telling of it, Apollodorus has acquired a memory seemingly identical with (and therefore really different from) his earlier knowledge of the symposium.

Aristophanes, once you grant the initial premises, everything follows from them with mad, relentless logic. The myth explains everything down to the most trivial details, such as the reason for the wrinkles around our navels. Aristophanes imbues his myth with comic grandeur and with true pathos in his description of the sphere men's quest to be reunited with their other halves after they've been split in two. His main contribution to the discussion is that Love is the *desire* for something—for wholeness and a lost state of happiness.

Following Aristophanes, Agathon the tragedian delivers a flashy, superficial speech in the artificial style of Gorgias, a Sicilian speechifier whose verbal pyrotechnics had electrified the Athenians a few years earlier. Silly as Agathon's speech is, it does add a new idea to the discussion: Love is the desire for *beauty*.

From the depths of Agathon's tawdry brilliance the dialogue rises in Socrates' speech to a pitch of splendor that would be hard to take if it were not offset by Socrates' ruse of presenting himself as the witless stooge of his all-wise mentoress, Diotima. Diotima treats the eager young Socrates much as Socrates treats his young victims. This graceful dodge of turning the tables on himself allows Socrates to atone for his sharp criticism of the other guests' speeches and for his rough treatment of Agathon in the preceding discussion. Socrates' stratagem also allows him to deliver his speech in the form of a dialogue and lends it a good-humored charm.

Love emerges from Socrates' speech as highly ambiguous: as neither good nor bad, beautiful nor ugly, wise nor foolish, mortal nor immortal, but rather as intermediate between these extremes. Love is desire: for something lacking or lost, as Aristophanes had said, and for beauty (equated, as usual, with the good), as Agathon had said. Since Love is shown to be the desire of possessing beauty *forever*, Love is also the desire for immortality.

So much for Love's nature and object. Socrates (or Diotima) next goes on to explain Love's function. He is a ladder, a necessary intermediary or implement that enables the soul to climb from deceitful appearance to absolute truth, an ascent called "education." The erotic ladder consists of a series of rungs leading from the physical to the spiritual, from the particular to the general, and ultimately from this world of ceaseless change and becoming to eternal being and truth.

The foot of the ladder rests on the earth; its top extends beyond the heavens into the realm of forms. Its bottom rung is the love of one particular, beautiful body. The next higher rung is the recognition of the beauty in all beautiful bodies. From bodies, the loving soul ascends to beautiful souls, to beautiful customs and laws, to beautiful studies and knowledge, until finally it reaches the highest, most beautiful knowledge of all: "the revelation of the beautiful itself" (211c). This is the form of beauty.

The driving force behind this arduous upward struggle is Love, the desire for beauty and immortality. The ardent soul gazes on both when it has climbed out of the body and ascended the ladder of Love. This longing contemplation of pure beauty is a foretaste of eternity, when the soul sufficiently purified by such contemplation in life is freed by death from the prison of the body and goes to dwell among the objects of its desire, and thus knows all truth and all beauty.

When the lover's soul has ascended to the contemplation of the beautiful itself, says Diotima, it has "almost reached the final goal" (211b)—"almost," because there are numerous other forms still to observe, above all the form of the Good, the source of all being, from which the other forms derive their existence (*Republic* 508, ff.); and "almost," because, as we learn from the *Phaedo*, in this life the soul can only *contemplate* the forms. Only after death will it *commune* with them.

Here, then, lies the supreme importance of Love. Love is the educator of the soul, the ladder that leads it out of the morass of the merely human and physical and sets it on its course to eternity. Socrates is right in presenting love of beauty as the intermediary that leads the soul upward, for love of beauty is innate in our souls and needs only to be nurtured and developed to make the soul strive upward and aspire beyond itself. In this sense, beauty is the most accessible of the forms, and human love, properly guided, can be the soul's first little step toward eternity.

The goal of Diotima's Love ladder is knowledge of eternal truth, which is wisdom. A true lover, therefore, is a lover of wisdom, for which the Greek word is "philosopher." Thus Diotima's erotic education is the education of the true philosopher.

We've come a long way from Phaedrus's "sense of shame" and Pausanias's "self-improvement." But the close of

Socrates' speech is too lofty to serve as a suitable ending for so earthy a thing as a drinking party. The dialogue must be brought back down to earth. Enter Alcibiades, drunk.

Alcibiades is a notorious figure in Athenian history. A rich aristocrat and nephew of Pericles, handsome, charming, dissolute, and unscrupulous, he was to play a role in politics as scandalous and disastrous as his love life. But that all lies in the future; Alcibiades did not make his political debut until 415 B.C., a few months after the dramatic date of the *Symposium*. Here he is still the handsome young man, whose excesses the other guests can still blame on the exuberance of youth. The reader, however, knows Alcibiades' subsequent career and therefore sees him in an ironic double light: as he is presented here, and as he was soon to be. Plato shows that despite Alcibiades' confusion and potential evil, he nevertheless recognizes and admires the good in Socrates.

In his speech, Alcibiades praises Socrates rather than Love. He portrays him much as Socrates had portrayed Love: as courageous, enduring, impoverished, ardently desirous of beauty but never possessed of it. Like Love, Socrates is a mass of contradictions and, therefore, elusive: Alcibiades began by enticing him like a loved one and ended up pursuing him like a lover. Socrates is also ambiguous; neither one thing nor another, but something in between. Alcibiades' simile, in which he compares Socrates to a satyr, is singularly apt. A satyr is a hybrid: half man, half beast, and also partly divine— in short, a monster, like Socrates and Love.

Socrates is like Love because he is a philosopher, which Diotima defined as one who *desires* wisdom and beauty but does not *possess* them (204a-b). He is also like Love because he serves as a handmaiden to Love. Socrates' discussions, which reduce his young partners to that state of ignorance and perplexity which they find so annoying, are really acts of love, performed in the service of Love. Socrates acts as a young man's guide who, as Diotima put it, "directs him properly" and gets him started up the ladder of Love. But before a young soul will attempt that ascent, it must desire to do so. And before it can desire to do so, it must be forced to recognize its ignorance—its lack of knowledge—because a person "can't desire what he doesn't think he lacks" (204a). This is just what Socrates' discussions do: They force his partners to recognize their ignorance and thus arouse in them the desire to know.

Thus, though the means that Socrates employs may strike his young victims as ambiguous and often unpleasant, the end is unambiguous and clear: The ultimate end is eternal truth, which is beauty. By setting young souls on their course to eternity, Socrates acts as a devotee of Love, whose ways, as he says, he "distinctively practices" (212b).

the *phaedo*

The *Phaedo* is more straightforward in structure than the *Symposium*, but its argument is quite complex. Dramatically, it follows the *Apology*, the account of Socrates' defense at his trial, and the *Crito*, which recounts his refusal to escape from prison a day or two before his execution. The dramatic date of the *Phaedo* is the year of Socrates' death, 399 B.C.

The *Phaedo* takes its title from its narrator, Phaedo of Elis, a young companion of Socrates who had been with him on his last day and who now, some time later, is on his way home from Athens to Elis. On the way he has stopped at the small town of Phlius to visit some philosophical friends. They have not yet heard the details of Socrates' death, and they press Phaedo for the story. Phaedo complies, and his account to Echecrates and some unnamed companions forms the main dialogue.

Socrates' last discussion with his friends falls into three main parts: (1) his defense of the cheerful attitude he takes toward death, (2) four arguments for the immortality of the soul, and (3) a great myth that describes the nature of the other world and the fate of the soul after death. The dialogue ends with a moving description of Socrates' death.

Socrates defends himself against the charge of "facing death lightly" (63b, ff.) by referring to the rewards that await the philosopher after death. The greatest is knowledge, the thing he has loved and pursued all his life. Knowledge, of course, is only of forms, and it can be obtained only by the soul, to which the body is merely a hindrance. Therefore the true philosopher always tries to separate his soul from his body as much as he can (by concentrating on the forms). But absolute separation of the soul from the body is death; hence philosophy is defined as the "practice of dying." A true philosopher, therefore, since he has spent his whole life practicing dying, does not fear death but instead looks forward to it as a release from the prison of the body. (The parallel between Socrates' confinement in prison and the soul's imprisonment in the body runs all through the *Phaedo.*) After death, the released soul will know all truth directly. Since the philosopher loves truth, he obviously also loves death and views life merely as a preparation for it.

Cebes objects (69e) that this is fine, but true only if the soul survives the body, which has not yet been established. This leads to the arguments for the immortality of the soul. Socrates realizes that these arguments do not constitute proofs—nonempirical phenomena do not admit of proof and must remain in the realm of belief—and he repeatedly emphasizes the tentative nature of his arguments: "Shall we . . . *tell stories* and try to find out whether this is *likely* to be true or not?" (70b). But he does think that they establish the likelihood of the soul's immortality, and he probably felt that the cumulative weight of the arguments amounted almost to certainty.

The first argument (70c-72d) strikes us as specious, but on Socratic premises it may be valid. It rests on an analogy from the generation of opposites: As the larger arises from the smaller and the smaller from the larger, so sleep comes from waking and waking from sleep; in the same way, death comes from life (an observable fact) and life from death. Therefore the soul is immortal. Even if we were to grant the initial premise for the sake of the argument (which we would be reluctant to do, since what Socrates calls "opposites" we call "relative terms"), we would still object that waking and sleep are not "opposites" in the sense of large and small, but rather changes of state. And the relation of waking and sleep to life and death is only metaphorical: A sleeping person's consciousness merely subsides temporarily; it later returns, and the sleeper wakes up. Death is a much more drastic change of state: Consciousness and the vital functions cease altogether and do not return. Death is not so much the opposite of life as the cessation or negation of life. The argument makes more sense, however, if one thinks in Socratic terms. If opposites are opposites because they partake of opposite forms, then they may reasonably be said to "come from" each other: The larger, which now partakes of largeness, must previously have been smaller, when it partook of smallness. In the same way, waking and sleep may well participate in opposite forms and "come from" each other, and so also for life and death. Socrates' way of thinking is not ours; but it could be right, and by its terms, these analogies are reasonable and more persuasive.

Socrates' second argument (72e-77a) is highly suggestive and, for all we know, it may be true. It depends on the "theory of recollection." The gist of it is this: The human mind seems to possess certain innate ideas not derivable from experience, such as "equality." The existence and origin of such ideas is hard to explain. A possible explanation of them is that our souls experienced true equality in a previous existence and bring a vague memory of it with them when they are born into this life. This dormant memory is then awakened when we encounter approximately equal things here and notice their similarity or dissimilarity to true equality. The same for justice, beauty, and all the other universals. What we call "learning," therefore, is actually recollection. And if we acquired in a previous life the knowledge that we now recollect, then obviously our souls must have existed before we were born. The forms too must exist, because it was from them, according to Socrates, that we derived this knowledge. (Of course this theory applies only to "necessary" knowledge, such as mathematics, not to "contingent" knowledge, such as history. Two plus two is always necessarily four, and everyone can know it. It is not a *necessary* fact that the Battle of Waterloo was fought in 1815, and Socrates could not know it.)

But this, as Simmias and Cebes point out (77a-c), is only half a demonstration. It demonstrates (conclusively, they believe) that the soul existed before birth, but not that it will exist after death. Socrates therefore passes on to his third argument (78b-84b), that the soul is indissoluble and, hence, immortal. Like the first argument, this one seems rather farfetched, but it gains credibility with the acceptance of the forms.

At this point (84d, ff.) Simmias and Cebes enter two resounding objections that strike the listeners as incontrovertible and reduce them to gibbering perplexity. Despite the listeners' apprehensions, however, Socrates easily disposes of the first objection (91d, ff.) by showing that it contradicts the theory of recollection, which both objectors accept. His refutation of Cebes' objection is interesting because Socrates casts it in the form of an autobiography in which he tells how as a young man he had studied natural science, and then gave it up when he discovered that the authorities could not agree on ultimate causes, and how he came upon the forms as the ultimate cause and dialectic as the means of gaining knowledge of them. This leads into the last argument (102a-107a), which circles back to the first to argue from opposites again. Although this argument is technically impressive, it is not very convincing.

Socrates follows his final argument with a grandiose myth, thus rounding off the intellectual speculation with a poetic, religious affirmation of faith. The arguments appeal to our intellects, the myth to our emotions and imaginations. The myth presents a detailed (yet only provisional) description of the other world ("over there") and of the soul's experiences after death. It thus recalls the myth of Er, which closes the *Republic*, though it differs from it in detail. With solemn grandeur it affirms that though Socrates cannot *prove* the soul's immortality, he nevertheless believes in it with unshakable conviction. The quiet death scene with which the *Phaedo* closes affirms the same thing, not on the plane of subtle argumentation or sweeping poetry, but on the humdrum and even squalid level of paltry human affairs. Socrates quits life as we feel he must have entered it: with a joke on his lips, a sly quip about "a rooster to Asclepius."

The page and section references printed in the margins of the text are those of the Stephanus edition, which are used universally for citing passages from Plato.

principal dates

(the order of the dialogues is uncertain
and the list is not exhaustive)

428 B.C.	Birth of Plato at Athens. Fourth year of Peloponnesian War (between Athens and Sparta)
423	Aristophanes' comedy *Clouds* performed (parody of Socrates)
416	Agathon presents his first tragedy, gives the party recounted in Plato's *Symposium*
415	Athens launches the Syracusan expedition, led by Alcibiades (who appears in the *Symposium*), Nicias, and Lamachus. Alcibiades recalled in disgrace
404	End of Peloponnesian War. Athens surrenders to Sparta. Reign of the "Thirty Tyrants"
403	Overthrow of the Thirty and restoration of the Athenian Democracy
399	Socrates' trial and execution for impiety and corrupting the youth (70 years old). Dramatic date of the *Phaedo*
399-387	Early dialogues: *Apology, Euthyphro, Crito, Laches, Carmides, Ion, Lysis, Protagoras, Gorgias*
387	Plato's first trip to Syracuse; friendship with Dion, son-in-law and brother-in-law of Dionysius I, tyrant of Syracuse
386	Foundation of Plato's Academy at Athens
386-367	Middle dialogues: *Meno, Cratylus, Euthydemus, Phaedo, Symposium, Menexenus, Republic, Phaedrus, Parmenides, Theaetetus*

The Symposium

APOLLODORUS: I should be able to tell you the story— 172
I've practiced it enough. Why, just the day before yesterday I
was going up to Athens from my home in Phalerum[1] when a
man I know saw me and called after me playfully: "Hey,
Apollodorus! Wait for me, you Phalerian!"

So I waited. He caught up with me and said: "Apollodorus,
I've been looking all over for you. I want to hear about that
party of Agathon's with Socrates and Alcibiades and all the b
rest—what were the love speeches like? Someone else told me
about them, but his story wasn't very clear. He had heard it
from Phoenix, Philip's son, and he said you knew about it
too. So tell me the whole thing. As Socrates' friend you're the
one to report what he says. But first, were you there?"

"The story couldn't have been very clear," I said, "if you
think the party was so recent that I could have been there." c

"That's the impression I got," he said.

"I don't see how, Glaucon," I said. "You know that
Agathon moved out of Athens years ago,[2] and I've been with
Socrates for less than three. Since then, I've been with him
every day and made it my business to know everything he says
and does. Before that, I just ran around in circles like you. I 173
thought I was doing something important and philosophy
was just a waste of time, but really I was a miserable fool—
like you."

"Stop joking and answer my question," he said. "When
was the party?"

[1] **A harbor** about three miles southwest of Athens. One must walk
"up" to reach the city.

[2] **Agathon** moved to Macedonia about 407 B.C. and died there about
401. The external dialogue therefore takes place about 402, "years"
after 407, but before 401 (since Agathon is spoken of as being still
alive).

1

"We were still children," I said. "Agathon had just won first prize with his first tragedy.[3] It was the day after he celebrated the victory with his players."

"That really was long ago," he said. "But who told you—Socrates?"

b   "No," I said, "the same one that told Phoenix: a fellow called Aristodemus of Cydathenaeum—a little man who always went barefoot. He had been there, and as far as I could tell, he was one of Socrates' most ardent lovers at the time. Of course I've checked some of the details with Socrates, and they agree with what Aristodemus said."

"Why not tell it to me then?" he said. "We may as well talk as we go into town."

c   So I told it and got some practice, as I said. I guess I can tell it again if you gentlemen really want to hear it. Philosophical talk ravishes me anyhow, besides being useful, and I love it as much when I'm talking as when I listen to somebody else. But your rich businessmen's talk makes me exasperated. I feel sorry for you as my friends because what you consider so

d   important is really just waste of time.

Now maybe you think that I'm a miserable dog. Well, I think so too. But I don't think you fellows are miserable—I know damn well you are!

COMPANION: You're always the same, Apollodorus. You insult everyone, including yourself, and you seem to think that everyone but Socrates is absolutely wretched. I don't know where you got the nickname "Maniac" from, but every time you open your mouth you surely act like one: You snap and snarl at your friends, at yourself—at everyone but Socrates.

e   APOLLODORUS: So you think this attitude proves I'm mad and out of tune?

COMPANION: Let's not argue about it now, Apollodorus. Please, just do as we asked and tell us those speeches.

174   APOLLODORUS: All right, they were something like this. But wait, I'll try to tell it all from the beginning, the way Aristodemus told it to me.

Well, Aristodemus said he ran into Socrates, freshly bathed

---

[3] **Greek dramatists** competed in the theater for first, second, and third prize. Agathon presented his first tragedy in 416 B.C.; he therefore gave his party about fourteen years before this telling of it.

and wearing fancy shoes instead of being barefoot. So he asked him where he was going all dressed up like that.

"To dinner at Agathon's," Socrates answered (said Aristodemus). "I didn't go to the victory celebration yesterday because I was afraid of the crowd, so I promised I'd come today. That's why I'm all dressed up: 'beauty to beauty.' Say, how do you feel about going to dinner uninvited?"   b

"However you say," I said (said Aristodemus).

"Come along then," said Socrates. "We'll pervert the old proverb: 'birds of a feather flock together.' Homer, you know, had the insolence to corrupt it completely. He made Agamemnon a great warrior but his brother Menelaus 'a soft   c
spearman.'⁴ Then, when Agamemnon was giving a feast, Menelaus came uninvited. So the poorer man went to the better man's feast. The result of course was that 'birds of a kind were caught in a bind.'"

"If I go, Socrates, I'm afraid I'll be following Menelaus's example instead of yours—a nobody going to an intellectual's feast. So think up a good defense because I won't admit that I came uninvited. I'll say you invited me."   d

"We'll put our heads together⁵ and figure something out on the way," said Socrates. "Let's go."

Their conversation was something like that, said Aristodemus, and then they left. But on the way Socrates somehow fell into thought and stopped. Aristodemus stopped too, but Socrates told him to go on ahead. So he did. But, he said, when he got to Agathon's place he found himself in an embarrassing situation: The door was open and a slave   e
rushed out and brought him in to the guests, who were just getting ready to eat. The moment Agathon saw him, he cried, "Aristodemus, hello! You're just in time for dinner. If you've come for anything else, you'll have to put it off. I was looking for you yesterday to give you an invitation, but I couldn't find you anywhere. But why didn't you bring Socrates?"

"I turned around," said Aristodemus, "and he wasn't following me. So I said that I *had* brought Socrates. In fact, he had brought me."

"Fine," said Agathon. "Where is he"

"He was right behind me. I wonder where he is."   175

---

⁴ **The phrase** is from *Iliad* 17.588. Menelaus comes uninvited in *Iliad* 2.402-410.

⁵ **A quotation** from *Iliad* 10.224.

He said Agathon turned to a slave: "Go look for him and bring him here, will you, boy? Aristodemus, please sit by Eryximachus."

Aristodemus said one of the boys brought water and helped him wash. Then the other boy returned and said, "That Socrates has gone into a neighbor's porch. He just stands there. When I called he wouldn't come."

"That's odd," Agathon replied (said Aristodemus). "Call him again and don't take no for an answer."

b "Leave him alone," I demanded (said Aristodemus). "This is a habit of his—he goes off and stands wherever he happens to be. I'm sure he'll be along soon if you leave him alone. Don't bother him."

"Well, whatever you say," Agathon replied (said Aristodemus). "Now, boys, please serve us. Do it however you like—the way you do when no one's standing over you, which is something that *I* would never do. Pretend that we are your
c guests and you have to please us and earn our compliments."

Then they ate, he said, but still no Socrates. Agathon suggested they send after him again, but Aristodemus said that he wouldn't let them. Socrates finally came in when they were half done with dinner. Considering his habits, he hadn't been away very long. "Come over here and sit by me," said Agathon—he was reclining alone on the right[6]—"I want

---

[6] **Guests reclined** in pairs on couches, with a small portable table for their food. The seating arrangement at Agathon's symposium was something like this:

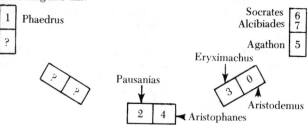

The far left, where Phaedrus is sitting, was the place of honor. The host usually took the lowest place, on the far right. Agathon occupies this position until Socrates arrives and reclines to his right. Alcibiades arrives late (212d) and sits between Agathon and Socrates. At the end (223b), Agathon moves to sit on Socrates' right. The speakers speak from left to right as indicated by the numbers. Aristophanes and Eryximachus exchange turns. Question marks indicate unnamed guests, whose speeches are not reported. Aristodemus, the narrator, apparently gives no speech.

to touch you and get some of that wisdom that came to you in the porch. I know you have it; you wouldn't have left till you did."   d

Aristodemus said Socrates sat down and said: "It would be nice if wisdom were as you say, Agathon, and it would flow from a full person to an emptier one when they touched, as water through wool from a full to an empty cup. If it did, I couldn't imagine anything more valuable than sitting by you   e because I know you'd fill me with beautiful wisdom. My wisdom's a poor, dubious thing—like a dream—but yours is brilliant and effusive. Why, just the day before yesterday you displayed your youthful brilliance and dazzled more than thirty thousand witnesses from all over Greece."[7]

"Don't be insolent, Socrates," Agathon replied (said Aristodemus). "In a little while you and I will settle this dispute over wisdom, and Dionysus will be the judge. But now eat your dinner."

He said Socrates reclined, and they finished their dinner.   176 Then they poured the libations, chanted the hymn to the gods, and performed the other rituals.[8] Next they turned to the drinking. Pausanias, he said, opened the discussion something like this: "Well, gentlemen, what's the easiest way to handle the drinking? To tell the truth, I'm still in bad shape from yesterday and could use a little recuperation. I think you could too, since most of you were here. So how shall we go about it?"   b

Aristophanes, said Aristodemus, replied: "As you say, Pausanias—the easiest way. I was completely stupefied yesterday."

"I agree," said Eryximaches, son of Acumenus. "Now how about Agathon? Are you up to it today?"

"No, I'm not up to it either."

[7] **By presenting** his prize-winning tragedy. "Youthful" contrasts Agathon's youth with Socrates' age (he was fifty-three in 416 B.C.). Dionysus, below, was the god of both wine and the drama.

[8] **A dinner** was distinct from a symposium, or drinking party, which now follows. The dinner was formally concluded by a hymn and libations to the gods. A symposium was governed by formal rules, which is why Pausanias asks about the drinking procedure. There was normally a "master of ceremonies," who prescribed the manner of drinking and the accompanying activities. Here Phaedrus serves as the leader until Alcibiades later (213e) appoints himself master of ceremonies.

c   "We would consider it an absolute godsend," observed Eryximachus (said Aristodemus), "—particularly Aristodemus, Phaedrus, and I—if you heavy drinkers were temporarily incapacitated, because we never have any capacity. I exempt Socrates from my remarks; he doesn't care one way or the other—either way will suit him. Now, since none of the present company seems particularly inclined to overindulge, this may be an auspicious occasion for me to explain the true nature of drink. The findings of medical

d science have convinced me that intoxication is detrimental to the health. I would never intentionally drink to excess or advise one of my patients to do so, especially if he still had a hangover from the previous day."

    "I always do whatever you say," interrupted Phaedrus the Myrrhinusian, "especially in medical matters. The others will too, if they have any sense."

e   So, said Aristodemus, everyone agreed to drink more for pleasure than to get drunk.

    "I take it we are resolved then," continued Eryximachus, "to drink only as much as we wish and to compel no one to drink more. I now move that we dismiss this flute girl who has just come in. She can play to herself or to the women inside while we spend the time in conversation. If you're wondering what kind, I've a proposal to make."

177 Aristodemus said they told him to make it.

    "The beginning of my speech," Eryximachus began (said Aristodemus), "is taken from Euripides' *Melanippe:*[9] 'Not mine the tale'—but Phaedrus's here. More than once Phaedrus has accosted me and indignantly complained: 'Isn't it a scandal, Eryximachus, that of all the poets who have written hymns and odes to the gods, not one has ever seen fit to compose a poem in honor of the great and venerable god of

b Love? And if you look through the works of the great sophists, like Prodicus, you'll find plenty of prose eulogies to Heracles and other heroes, but not a single one to Love. That's outrageous enough, but recently I came across a book by some sophist who had composed a marvelous encomium

c on—the usefulness of salt! About drivel like that they make a terrible fuss, but not one soul has yet had the nerve to write a decent hymn to Love. A god is neglected while salt gets extolled to the skies!'

[9] **A lost tragedy.** Prodicus, below, was a famous sophist whose specialty was the precise definition of words.

"I move Phaedrus's point as well taken. I would therefore like to favor him publicly by suggesting this as a fitting occasion to adorn the neglected god. If that seems congenial   d
to you, I'm sure we'll find sufficient entertainment in speeches. Here is my proposal: Each of us will give a speech—as beautiful as he can make it—in praise of Love. We shall go from left to right, beginning with Phaedrus, who not only is sitting the first on the left, but is also the father of the speech."

"No one will vote against you, Eryximachus," said Socrates (according to Aristodemus). "I hardly could, because love is the only thing that I claim to know. Neither could Agathon and Pausanias, and certainly not Aristophanes, who   e
devotes all his time to Dionysus[10] and Aphrodite. As far as I can see, we'll all second your proposal, even if it won't be a fair contest for us who speak last. But if the first speakers do a good job, we'll be satisfied. So go ahead, Phaedrus, and good luck."

Aristodemus said the others concurred and urged Phaedrus to begin.

Now Aristodemus couldn't remember every speech in   178
detail, and I can't remember everything he told me. But I'll relate the main points of each speech I consider worth telling.

SPEECH OF PHAEDRUS

Well, as I said, Phaedrus was the first speaker. Aristodemus said he opened with something about Love being a great god, amazing among gods and men. "The reasons are many," he said, "but chief is his birth. Love is revered as the most ancient of gods. Here is my proof: Love has no parents. No one,   b
layman or poet, has ever disputed that. Hesiod, in fact, confirms it when he says that first Chaos was born, and then 'Broad-bosomed Earth, sure, eternal foundation of all,/ and Love.'[11] Acusilaus agrees that after Chaos these two, Earth and Love, were born. And Parmenides says that Birth 'Planned Love as first of all the gods.' Thus from all sides it is   c
agreed that Love is an ancient and venerable god.

[10] As patron god of the theater. Aphrodite was the goddess of love.
[11] The quotation is from *Theogony* 117. Acusilaus was a poet whose works are lost. Parmenides was an early fifth-century philosopher who believed that "everything is one." Therefore there can be no change or plurality in the real world. The visible world of change is an illusion.

"Being ancient and venerable, Love is the source of great blessings to man. And the greatest blessing I can name is for a young boy to find a good lover and a lover a good boy. To live a beautiful life a man must be guided by a principle which nothing—neither birth, nor wealth, nor office—can so

d beautifully inspire as Love. This principle is shame for the shameful and emulation of the beautiful. Without that, neither a city nor an individual can do anything beautiful or great. Suppose a man in love is caught doing something shameful or suffering it because he's too cowardly to resist: I say he'll be more distressed if seen by his loved one than if by a

e friend or even his father. The same for a loved one—he'll be terribly ashamed if his lover sees him do something ugly.

"If there were a way to give birth to a state or an army of nothing but lovers and loved ones who would shun shameful activity while vying with each other for honor, that would be

179 the best possible organization, and in battle a few such men could defeat practically the whole world. A loving man would never throw away his sword or break ranks if he knew his loved one would see him; he'd rather die a thousand deaths. As for abandoning his loved one or not helping him in danger, no one is so base that Love cannot inspire him with

b courage, as though he were noble by nature. In short, the effect Homer describes of 'a god breathing might'[12] into heroes is Love's effect upon lovers, brought forth from himself.

"And only lovers—not only men, but women too—will die for the sake of another. Alcestis, daughter of Pelias, provides sufficient proof of that for us Greeks. She was the only one willing to die for her husband, and though his parents still

c lived, she so far excelled them in affection because of Love that she showed them to be strangers to their son and parents only in name. So beautiful was this act judged to be by both gods and men that the gods granted Alcestis a favor they've conferred upon only a tiny number of all those who have done beautiful deeds: Out of admiration for her they allowed

d her soul to return from the dead. Thus even gods award the highest honors to courage and diligence in Love.

---

[12] **The reference** is to *Iliad* 10.482, 15.60, etc. Alcestis, below, is the heroine of Euripides' *Alcestis*. She makes a bargain with Death to die in place of her husband Admetus so that he may go on living.

"But Orpheus,[13] son of Oeagrus, was sent back from Hades undone. He had gone for his wife, but the gods gave him only a phantom because they considered him a weakling (he was merely a minstrel) who didn't dare to die for love, like Alcestis, but had sneaked into Hades alive. Therefore they justly made his death be delivered by women; they didn't honor him and send him to the Isles of the Blest, as they did   e
Achilles, Thetis' son. Achilles had learned from his mother that he would die at Troy if he killed Hector; if not, he would die at home of old age. Nevertheless, he dared to avenge his lover Patroclus and chose not merely to die in his place but to   180
follow him into death. Hence the gods' extreme admiration and honor for him: he had considered his lover to be so important.

"Aeschylus talks nonsense when he says Achilles was Patroclus's lover rather than his loved one.[14] Achilles was more beautiful than Patroclus or any hero, much younger and still beardless, as Homer says. Much as the gods honor excellence[15] in love, they are truly amazed, astounded, and   b
happy at the affection of a loved one—more so than at the

[13] **A legendary musician.** When his wife Eurydice died, Orpheus persuaded the lord of the underworld to allow him to bring her back, on condition that he not look back at her until they reached the upper world. He did look back and so lost her. Phaedrus changes the story for his own purposes. The scene below between Achilles and his mother Thetis is from *Iliad* 18.73-137. Achilles is placed on the Isles of the Blest by Pindar in *Olympian* 2.68-83.

[14] In the *Myrmidons*, a lost tragedy. As usual in Plato, love is presented primarily as pederastic: the love between a man and a youth. The distinction made here and throughout the dialogue between "lover" and "loved one" is common in Greek, though it may puzzle an English reader. We tend to emphasize the similarity and equality that exists between (as we say) "a pair of lovers." The Greeks, however, emphasized the difference and disparity between them. They thought of the relationship as resembling that between master and slave; the loved one has the power to control the one who loves him. There must always be a lover and a loved one; never two lovers (impossible by definition). The reference to Homer, which follows, is to *Iliad* 2.673 and 11.786.

[15] *Arete*, traditionally translated as "virtue." Its basic sense is excellence or ability at something—being good at it. Though strictly a limited term (excellence *at* something), Plato tends to make it absolute: the excellence or virtue that makes any thing distinctively that which it is, especially that which makes a man a man.

lover's affection for him. The lover is more divine than the loved one; he is possessed by a god. That's why the gods honored Achilles more than Alcestis and sent him to the Isles of the Blest.

"Thus I maintain that Love is the most ancient and honored of gods, most effective in providing excellence and happiness for all men, living and dead."

c   Phaedrus's speech was something like that, said Aristodemus, and then came several speeches that he couldn't remember very well. So he skipped them and went on to the speech of Pausanias.

SPEECH OF PAUSANIAS

Pausanias (said Aristodemus) began like this: "Phaedrus, I think your proposal was bad, to eulogize Love in this simple way. If Love were one, it would be all right. But Love is not one. Since he is not one, the proper way to proceed is first to
d   proclaim which Love to praise. I shall try to set this straight by telling first which Love to praise and then by praising him as he deserves.

"We all know: no Love, no Aphrodite.[16] If she were one, Love were one. But she is two, so Love is two. Of course there are two Aphrodites. The older is the motherless daughter of Uranus. We call her Uranian Aphrodite. The younger is the daughter of Zeus and Dione. We call her Common Aphrodite.
e   We're thus compelled to call the Love who works with the first goddess Heavenly Love, the other Common Love. We must properly praise all the gods, but I must try to present this pair's prerogatives.

"Every act is neutral, neither beautiful nor ugly in itself.
181 Take what we're doing—drinking, singing, or speaking: None in itself is beautiful. Beauty only comes from doing, the way an act is done. If done properly, it's beautiful, otherwise not. So for loving and Love: Not all are beautiful and worth our praise; only the one who turns us to beautiful loving.

"Common Love is truly common and doesn't care what he
b   does. This is the Love that worthless people love. These love

[16] **I.e., "no love, no sex."** Aphrodite was the goddess of sexual love and so is often used as a synonym for sex. The dual mythology of Love and Aphrodite which follows is probably Plato's own invention. Uranus is Heaven (one of the Titans, or elder gods). "Uranian" is therefore synonymous with "Heavenly."

women as much as boys, their bodies more than their souls, and they even prefer their loved ones to be perfectly mindless because all they want is action, regardless of how it's done. Hence they do whatever they feel like, indifferent to good and bad. Their Love comes from the young goddess who shared at birth in both the male and the female. But Heavenly Love loves boys and comes from the Aphrodite who shared not in the female but only in the male and who is older and free from insolence. Hence men fired by that Love pursue males; they dote on the naturally strong and intelligent. Even in pederasty you can spot the lovers driven by pure Heavenly Love. They don't love young boys but wait till they start to have sense, which is when they begin to get their first beard.

"I think a lover who starts with a boy at that age shows his true intent: to spend his life with him. He doesn't deceive a senseless child, then laugh and flit off in contempt to some other young thing. There should be a law against loving young boys; it would save a lot of energy from being squandered on uncertain affairs. It's always uncertain how a young boy will turn out—sound in mind and body or not. Good men impose this law on themselves, but we should force the herd to obey it too, just as we keep them, as far as we can, from making love to free-born women. These are the lovers that give Love a bad name: People look at them and see their unfairness and lack of tact and dare to call it ugly to gratify[17] lovers. You'd hardly think anyone could criticize this or anything else that's done in a fair, orderly way.

"The love customs in most states are easy to grasp; they're simple. But here they're complex. In Elis, Boeotia,[18] and wherever people are unskilled at speech, they simply call gratifying a lover beautiful. No one there would call it ugly, mainly so they won't have to use words to persuade the young men, which they couldn't do anyway. But in Ionia and other places controlled by the Persians they regard gratifying lovers as ugly. These barbarians even consider sports and philosophy shameful, owing to their despotic government.

---

[17] To "gratify" or "favor" a lover is a polite euphemism for sexual intercourse.

[18] **Elis and Boeotia** were considered by the Athenians to be backwater areas, and the Boeotians were considered particularly stupid. Ionia, below, was the Greek Asia Minor seacoast. Being close to Persia, it was often under Persian domination.

c Absolute rulers could hardly tolerate big ideas, strong friendships, and tight associations among their subjects— precisely the things that sports and philosophy, but especially Love, tend to produce. The Athenian tyrants[19] learned that the hard way: Aristogiton and Harmodius had such a solid friendship that it brought down their government. So wherever custom calls it ugly to gratify
d lovers, it rests on the lawmakers' malice, the rulers' greed, and the subjects' cowardice. Where it proclaims it a simple good, the law stems from the mental indolence of its makers.

"But we have a beautiful custom and, as I said, one not easy to grasp. Reflect how we value open love above the furtive kind, especially the love of noble, aristocratic young men (even if they're homlier than the others); how much encouragement a lover gets from all sides (hardly as though loving were regarded as shameful!); how a conquest enhances
e his reputation while failure destroys it; how, in attempting a seduction, a lover receives permission to do things that would
183 bring him the vilest disgrace if attempted for any other motive but love—if, say, a man wanted money or office or power from someone and stooped to do the things that lovers do to their sweethearts—making pleas and entreaties, swearing eternal vows, sleeping on their doorsteps, offering to be their slaves and to do things for them that no real slave would ever do—why, his friends and enemies alike would restrain him,
b his friends by rebuking him and feeling ashamed, his enemies by denouncing him as a servile, groveling flatterer, whereas a lover who does these very same things is not merely excused but set above criticism, as though seduction were considered a beautiful thing, while the strangest thing of all, according to public opinion, is that the gods forgive a lover—and no one else—for breaking an oath because 'a sex oath is no oath';
c therefore, so our custom declares, both gods and men grant a lover complete license to do whatever he wants—reflect upon that, and you'll be forced to conclude that our custom creates a perfect climate for both loving and being friendly to lovers. But when fathers assign slaves to keep their sons from talking to lovers, and when a boy's friends criticize him
d if they see him talking to one, and when these boys' elders

---

[19] **Athens** was ruled by tyrants from 546 to 510 B.C. In 514, Harmodius and Aristogiton assassinated the tyrant's brother and so helped bring down the tyranny.

don't even try to control them or scold them for their vicious tongues—when you see things like that, you might well conclude that the custom here is the ugliest of all.

"The truth, I believe, is as I said at the start: gratifying a lover is not a simple act, beautiful or ugly in itself. It depends how it's done: It's beautiful if done beautifully, ugly if not. Ugly means gratifying a base lover basely; beautiful means gratifying a good lover well. A base lover is that common lover, who loves the body more than the soul; he's fickle because what he loves is unstable. When the bloom leaves the body he loves, he 'flutters away'[20] and puts all his oaths and promises to shame. But the lover of character is a lover for life, because he's welded to that which is stable.

"Our custom well tests these two types of lover and says, 'Gratify this type but shun the other.' It incites the lover to chase, the beloved to flee, that the race may test them and expose which class each belongs to. And it denounces as ugly a loved one's rapid submission. Time should pass, for time tests most things well. Nor must a loved one submit for money or political power, whether beaten into cringing submission by cruelty he cannot endure or lured by financial or political favors he fails to despise. We believe that nothing is certain or stable about money and power except their natural inability to engender noble friendship.

"Our custom leaves only one path open for loved ones to gratify lovers. Just as it permits lovers to be the willing slaves of their loved ones in anything without being denounced as servile flatterers, so it permits loved ones to perform only one kind of voluntary service that will keep them from being denounced. That is service for excellence. Our custom states that if one person desires to serve another erotically to become a better man through him, either in knowledge or in some other part of excellence, such voluntary slavery is neither servile nor ugly.

"These two customs—the first concerning boy love, the second concerning knowledge and other excellence—must both contribute to the same end if gratifying a lover is to turn out well. When lover and loved one, each observing his proper custom, come together for the same end—the lover rightly serving his loved one to gain his permission, the loved one rightly permitting what may be permitted to one that can

[20] These words are used of a dream in *Iliad* 2.71.

e make him knowing and good—and when the lover can
provide the intelligence and excellence the loved one needs to
get knowledge and education, it is then and only then—at the
conjunction of those two customs contributing to a common
end—that gratifying a lover turns out beautiful.

185 "In this situation even getting deceived brings no shame,
whereas gratifying a lover for any other motive is ugly
whether you're deceived or not. Suppose a boy gratifies a rich
lover for money and then gets cheated out of it when the lover
is exposed as poor. That's ugly even though the boy was
deceived. He has betrayed his true nature—a willingness to do
anything for money; and that's not beautiful. But the
deception is beautiful if, for the sake of self-improvement, a
boy favors a lover who seems good and then finds himself
deceived when his lover is exposed as bad and lacking
b excellence. He too has revealed his true nature—eagerness to
do anything for anyone for the sake of excellence and
becoming a better man; and that's the most beautiful thing
there is.

"Thus gratifying lovers for excellence is utterly beautiful.
This is the Heavenly Love of the Uranian goddess, valuable
to both states and individuals, because he forces the lover and
c loved one each to care for his own excellence. All other loves
come from Common Aphrodite. That, Phaedrus," he said,
"is my impromptu presentation in praise of Love."

Pausanias paused (I learned to speak jingles like that from
the sophists), and Aristodemus said it was Aristophanes'
turn. But he had the hiccups from "repletion" or something
and couldn't give a speech, so he turned to Eryximachus the
doctor, who was reclining beside him, and said:
"Eryximachus, if you were a friend, you'd either stop my
hiccups or speak in my place until they stop by themselves."

"I shall do both," Eryximachus said. "I'll take your turn
and when your indisposition abates you may take mine. As I
speak, refrain from breathing awhile and the agitation
e should cease. If not, gargle with water. If they remain violent,
tickle your nose with something to induce sneezing. Do that
once or twice and they'll relent, no matter how severe they
may be."

"Speak," said Aristophanes. "I'll try it."

SPEECH OF ERYXIMACHUS

"Well now, Pausanias seems to have charged into his speech well enough but didn't really end it, so it's up to me to apply a proper ending. I think he made a useful distinction in distinguishing double Love. But I believe one may observe from my science, medicine, that Love operates not only in human souls upon beautiful young men, but in and upon everything—in all living bodies and plants and in practically all that exists: Love is a great and marvelous god whose influence extends to all things human and divine.

186

b

"I shall begin with medicine, so I may venerate my science as well as the god. Now the nature of the body displays double love. Physical illness and health are admittedly different and unlike, and unlikes desire and love different things. So one kind of love exists in a healthy body, another exists in a sick. As Pausanias just said about people—it is beautiful to gratify good men but ugly to gratify lechers—so also with bodies: it is beautiful, even necessary, to gratify the good in each body (such gratification is called medicine), but ugly to gratify the sick and the bad, which we must in fact frustrate to become good technicians. Now medicine, briefly defined, is the science of bodily loves as they pertain to repletion and evacuation, and a man who can diagnose the beautiful love and the ugly will be a good diagnostician, while one who can exchange the one for the other and apply love where it is needed and excise it from where it doesn't belong will be a good practitioner. He must also, of course, be able to reconcile the body's hostile elements and cause them to love one another. The most hostile are opposites like the hot and the cold, the wet and the dry, the bitter and the sweet. According to our poets here—[21]and I for one believe them— Asclepius, our patron, knew how to apply love and affinity to these opposites and so founded my science.

c

d

e

"This Love, I maintain, charts the whole course of medicine and also of athletics and agriculture. It will be obvious to even a casual observer that the same is true of music, as Heraclitus perhaps tried to say, though he didn't choose his words very well. 'The One,' he says, 'differs from

187

---

[21] **I.e., Agathon and Aristophanes.** Asclepius was the god of medicine.

Plato

itself and agrees, like the harmony of a lyre and bow.'[22] But it is quite absurd to say that harmony differs from itself or consists of elements which currently differ. Perhaps he was trying to say that a harmony comes from elements which previously differed—high and low notes—but which have been brought to agreement by the science of music. It could hardly come from notes that currently differ. A harmony is a concord and a concord an agreement, and you can never have agreement between parties as long as they differ. Nor can you harmonize elements that differ or disagree. So with rhythm: It comes from elements which previously differed—fast and slow beats—and which later are made to agree. Here it is music, as before it was medicine, that makes all these opposites agree by introducing love and affinity among them. So music is the science of love as it pertains to harmony and rhythm. In the theoretical constitution of harmony and rhythm the love elements are easy to diagnose and double love doesn't yet come in. But applying rhythm and harmony for people's benefit, either by creating music—which is called composition—or by properly performing songs already composed—called education—[23]is difficult and calls for a skilled technician.

"So again the conclusion comes round: We must gratify orderly men and try to make orderly those who are not, preserving their love, which is the beautiful, Heavenly Love who comes from the Uranian Muse. Common Love comes from the Muse of popular music, and one must prescribe him cautiously in only small doses so people may enjoy him without catching lechery, just as in my profession one must be careful about diet, so that people may enjoy food without

---

[22] **Heraclitus** was an early fifth-century philosopher who believed that everything is in flux and strife; the only thing permanent is change. The quotation is abridged by Plato. In full it reads: "It is at variance and yet agrees with itself; there is a back-stretched connection, as in the lyre and bow." This seems to mean that reality exists because of a constant internal tension and strife, just as a bow may be said to exist because of the tension between bow and string. Break the string and you no longer have a bow but only its constituents. Eryximachus gets confused because he takes the word *harmony* in its later musical sense rather than in its earlier sense of "connection," which Heraclitus intended.

[23] **This is not arbitrary;** in Greek "music" also means "education."

harming their health. Thus in music and medicine and all technical skills, human and divine, we must try to preserve, insofar as we can, both of these Loves. For both are in all.

"Even the arrangement of the seasons is filled with both of these Loves, and when the opposites I mentioned earlier encounter orderly Love and attain a temperate, harmonious blending, they come bearing health and good fellowship to men, animals, and crops, and there is justice. But when the insolent Love dominates the seasons, he destroys everything and injustice is unleashed. Such conditions are conducive to plagues and other discordant diseases that afflict both animals and crops. Frost, hail, and blight are bred from the disorder and greed of these love forces, the science of which we call astronomy, because it studies the movements of stars and the seasons of the year.

"Finally we come to sacrifice and prophecy—the communion of gods and men—which pertain solely to the preservation and cure of Love. All kinds of impiety, toward gods and one's parents, living or dead, tend to occur when people fail in all of their works to honor, gratify, and venerate the orderly Love over the other. So prophecy is the technique charged with the examination and cure of these Loves, as the science of friendship between gods and men, which studies those principles of human love that influence piety and righteousness.

"Thus total Love has wide and extensive or, more succinctly, total power, and the Love concerned for the good and consummated with temperance and justice among both us and the gods has the greatest power of all: He provides total happiness and makes us capable of friendship and social intercourse with one another and with those greater than us, the gods.

"Now perhaps in my eulogy I've overlooked much, but it wasn't intentional. And it's your task, Aristophanes, to fill in whatever I may have missed. Or if you intend to speak differently, do—your hiccups seem to have stopped."

"Yes," admitted Aristophanes (said Aristodemus), "but not till I gave them the sneeze treatment. I'm amazed that my body's 'orderly love' desires such disgusting noises and gurgles. But it must; they stopped as soon as I sneezed."

"Be careful, my friend," said Eryximahcus. "If you intend to make jokes, you'll force me to censor your speech to make sure you don't try to be funny. So it's up to you if you want to be left in peace."

Aristophanes laughed: "You're right, Eryximachus. I take back what I said. Don't watch me; I'm nervous about my speech. Not that I may say something funny—that would be profitable and native to my Muse—but something ridiculous."

"You can't take a cheap shot at me and get away with it, Aristophanes. Watch what you say—I'll hold you
c   responsible for it. But if I like your speech, I may let you go."

SPEECH OF ARISTOPHANES

"Yes, Eryximachus, I will speak differently from you and Pausanias. You see, I don't think men realize the power of Love. If they did, they'd make him the fine temples, altars, and sacrifices he deserves, not neglect him as they do. Of all
d   the gods Love is the most concerned for our welfare; he is our ally who heals those wounds which, if once cured, would bring mankind perfect happiness. I shall therefore try to initiate you into his power, and you shall go out and teach others.

"First I must teach you about man's nature and its sufferings. Originally our nature was quite different than now. First of all, there were three sexes instead of just two.
e   Besides the male and the female there was a third sex that shared in the traits of both of the others. This was once a real sex, but its form disappeared and only its name—hermaphrodite—now remains, as a term of reproach.

"Originally every man was whole, and shaped like a sphere. His chest and back formed a circle, he had four arms,
190 four legs, and one head with two identical faces facing in opposite ways. As you can imagine, his ears numbered four, his genitals two, and so on for the rest. He walked upright like us and could go in either direction. But whenever he was in a hurry, he would throw his arms and his legs straight out from his body, turn cartwheels like an acrobat, and with eight limbs to support him, spin quickly to wherever he wanted to go.

"Here is the reason for the three sexes and the forms that
b   they took: The male was descended from the Sun, the female from the Earth, and the sex that shared in both came from the Moon, who shares in both the Sun and the Earth. Original man was spherical and his gait circular like his divine parents. These men had terrible strength and mighty ambitions, so that what Homer says of the Giants Ephialtes

and Otus[24] is said also of them: they attempted to scale heaven and make an attack on the gods.

"Zeus and the other gods held a conference to decide what   c
to do. It ended in frustration. They couldn't blast men with lightning, as they had the Giants, and eliminate the race—that would also eliminate the honors and sacrifices that they got from them. But they couldn't tolerate this outrage either.

"Zeus thought long, then had an idea: 'I think I've found a scheme,' he said, 'to foil this nefarious plot and still let men live. We'll cut them in half and kill two birds with one stone: d
They'll be weaker and also more useful to us because there'll be twice as many of them. Let 'em walk on two legs. And if they still don't keep the peace,' he thundered, 'I'll sunder them again, by god, and they can hop around on one leg, like sack-racers!'[25]

"With that Zeus split men the way you cut crab apples for pickling or slice a hard-boiled egg with a hair. As he did, he   e
told Apollo to twist their heads around toward the wound so that man would always have to face his cut side and behave in a more orderly way. Then he told him to heal the wounds. So Apollo turned the heads around and then pulled in the skin from all sides toward what we now call the belly, the way you pull in a purse with its drawstrings. He drew it up tight to make a little mouth in the middle and then tied it off. This is what we now call the navel. Then he propped up the chest   191
with ribs and smoothed out the wrinkles, using a tool like shoemakers use to smooth out wrinkles in leather. But he left a few wrinkles around the belly-button as a reminder of our ancient wound.

"After man's nature had been split, each half longed for its other, and they would come together, throw their arms around each other and entwine because they craved to grow back together again. And since each refused to do anything apart from the other, they began to die of starvation and   b
general indolence. Whenever one half would die, the survivor would seek out another half and entwine with it, whether it happened to be the half of a whole women—this half is what

[24] **The reference** is to *Odyssey* 11.307-20.
[25] **Literally:** "hop on greased wine skins," a reference to a contest held at a country festival (the "Ascolia"). The contestants apparently had their legs tied together, and the contest was similar to a sack race.

we now call a woman—or of a man. Thus man was becoming
extinct.

"But Zeus pitied man and cooked up another scheme: He
moved the genitals around to the front. Till then they'd been
in the back because they'd been on the outside before, and

c   men had conceived not on each other but on the earth, like
grasshoppers. But Zeus put the genitals in front and made
men conceive on each other, the male on the female, and
again killed two birds with one stone: If a man had intercourse with a woman, she'd conceive and perpetuate the race;
if with a man, they'd at least be repleted, stop, and go back to
work to take care of the other needs of life. It was then that

d   man was endowed with mutual Love, the restorer of our
original nature who attempts to make one out of two and heal
our human condition.

"Thus we're each but the token of a man—cut in half the
way parting friends break dice in half so they can recognize
each other again by matching the pieces. Each of us is
searching for his matching token. Men cut from the common
sex—which was then called hermaphrodite—love women.

e   Ladies' men and most seducers come from this sex, as do men-
hungry women, the *femmes fatales*. Women who come from
the original female are lesbians, more interested in women
than in men. Men cut from the original male pursue males.
As boys they love men and enjoy entwining and sleeping with

192 them because they themselves are slices of the male. These are
the best young men, by nature the most masculine. Those
who say they are shameless lie. They sleep with men not out
of shamelessness but out of boldness, manliness, and courage,
because they cherish what resembles themselves. Here is my
proof: These are the only boys who grow up fit for politics.

b   When such a man comes of age, he becomes a lover of boys,
uninterested in marriage and raising a family, which he does
only because custom demands it. As one completely devoted
to boy love and male companionship, he'd prefer to stay
single and live with boys, cherishing his own kind.

"Now when a person, boy lover or anyone else, finds his
other half, an amazing love, kinship, and passion seizes them

c   and makes them unwilling to part from each other for even a
little while. These are the lovers who stay together for life,
though even they couldn't say what it is that they want from
each other. No one would think it was sex that bound them in
such deep and serious joy. Clearly their soul desires

something else, but it can't say what, though it hints at it   d
darkly, in riddles.

"Suppose while two lovers were lying embraced,
Hephaestus[26] should appear to them with his tools and ask:
'What is it, O mortals, you want from each other?' And if they
were perplexed he would say: 'Is it this—to be joined so
closely that you never shall part by night or by day? If so, I'm
here to melt you and weld you together, and make you one out   e
of two so you may live all your life together as one and die all
your death together in Hades as one rather than two. —Well?
Is that what you love? Will that satisfy you?'

"We all know that no lover would refuse such an offer.
He'd believe he had heard just what he had always desired: to
melt and merge with his loved one and become one out of
two. This is because our original nature was one and we were
whole. Our name for this desire and pursuit after wholeness is
'love.'

"Originally, I say, we were one, but because of our injustice   193
the gods dispersed and resettled us, as the Spartans did the
Arcadians. And if we don't behave in an orderly way, we must
fear that the gods may cut us in half again and make us run
around like relief figures carved on monuments—split down
the middle through the nose, like fish fillets. Therefore every
man must exhort every other to show reverence toward the
gods; that we may avoid such a fate, and with Love as our   b
leader and guide, attain what we truly desire. Let no man,
therefore, act contrary to Love—he does so who angers the
gods—but let us make up with him and be friends and so find
our own proper loved ones, which is a thing that now
happens to only a few.

"I hope Eryximachus doesn't make fun of my speech and
accuse me of referring to Pausanias and Agathon. Perhaps
they are slices of the male and naturally masculine. But I refer   c
to all men and all women when I say that the whole human
race will be happy if each of us consummates his love by
finding his loved one and returning with him to our original
condition. If this is the best condition, then whichever of us
has come the closest to it—by finding the loved one who
matches his nature—must be the best of us all. And if we
would praise the god who is the cause of this boon, we will
justly sing paeans to Love, who for the present performs a   d

---

[26] The blacksmith god.

great service by bringing us together with our own and who holds out for the future the greatest hope that if we show reverence toward the gods, he will heal our ancient wounds, restore our pristine nature, and so make us blessed and happy again.

"That, Eryximachus, is my speech about Love—different from yours. Please don't make fun of it, so we can hear what the others will say. I guess I should say 'the other two,' because only Agathon and Socrates are left."

e

"Oh, I shan't," Eryximachus assured him (said Aristodemus). "I found it quite pleasant. If I weren't aware that Socrates and Agathon are experts on love, I'd be terribly anxious for them after hearing so many different speeches on the subject. But as it is, I'm quite optimistic."

194 "You competed very well yourself, Eryximachus," said Socrates (according to Aristodemus). "But if you were in my place, or rather in the place I'll undoubtedly be after Agathon has made his beautiful speech, you'd be as helpless and terrified as I am."

"Socrates," said Agathon, "you're trying to jinx me by making me think my audience has great expectations of me as a clever speaker."

"I saw your proud self-assurance the other day, Agathon, as
b you mounted the stage with your actors. You looked out over that huge crowd before you presented your play and didn't show the least sign of nervousness. After seeing that, I'd be pretty forgetful if I thought you'd be upset now in front of our little group."

"Do you think I'm so stage-struck that I don't even know a small audience of intellectuals is more frightening to a sensible man than a crowd of fools?"

c "I'm sure I'd be making a mistake if I thought you at all unsophisticated, Agathon. I know if you found some people you thought clever, you'd care more about them than about the crowd. But that leaves us out, I'm afraid: we were there the other day and were part of the crowd. But if you found some others who were clever, you'd probably feel ashamed around them if you did something that you thought was shameful. Isn't that so?"

"Yes," replied Agathon (said Aristodemus).

"But you wouldn't be ashamed around the crowd if you did something that you thought was shameful?"

d But Phaedrus, Aristodemus said, interrupted them: "Don't

answer him, Agathon. If you do, he won't care about anything as long as he has someone to talk to—especially if that someone is handsome. I enjoy listening to Socrates' discussions, but I have to look after the Love speeches and make sure I get one from each of you. So each give a speech and then you can have a discussion."

"You're right, Phaedrus," said Agathon, "—nothing will stop me. There'll be plenty of opportunities later for discussions with Socrates."   e

SPEECH OF AGATHON

"First I shall seek to tell how to speak and then speak. Of the previous speakers none, it seems, celebrated the god but felicitated man for the goods of which the god is the cause. But what sort is the god who confers all those gifts no one has said. There's but one right way to make any eulogy on any   195 subject: to expound in a speech what sort of cause of what sort of effects the subject of that eulogy is. So with Love: It's right to praise him first as he is, then his gifts.

"Of all the happy gods, I say—may divine Right and Wrath permit me to say!—the happiest is Love, being most beautiful and best. He is most beautiful thus: First, Phaedrus, he is youngest of all. Of this he himself provides fairest proof,   b by fleeing in fear from old age—a very fast thing, it is clear, since it comes upon us quicker than it ought. Love by nature hates old age and comes not within its reach. But with the young he consorts and ever resorts. And it was truly said of old: Like ever consorts with its like.

"Though agreeing with Phaedrus in much, here I do not. Love's not older than Cronus and Iapetus,[27] but youngest, say I, of the gods, and remains ever so. The old horrors told of the   c gods by Hesiod and Parmenides, if they speak true, occurred not under Love but Necessity. The gods would never have chained or castrated each other or done those other violent deeds, had Love been with them. Peace and friendship had reigned, as now, since Love has ruled as their king.

"Young then he is, and gentle. It would take a poet like Homer to reveal this god's gentleness. Homer calls Ruin a   d

[27] **Both Titans** or elder gods. Cronus castrated his father Uranus and seized control of the universe, and Zeus in turn deposed Cronus (his father) and chained him in Tartarus. These are the "horrors" mentioned below.

goddess and gentle—gentle at least in her feet: 'And gentle her feet; for not o'er the glebe/does she glide, but treads on the heads of men.'[28] A beautiful proof this would seem of Ruin's gentleness, who treads not on the rough but the soft. The

e   same proof may suffice to show Love as gentle. For he treads not upon earth nor even on heads—which are not very soft—but in the softest of the soft he treads as well as dwells. In the dispositions and souls of gods and men he founds his abode, though not in all without discrimination; should he find a soul with a rough disposition he leaves; if soft, he settles. And clinging always in all ways to the softest of the soft, he must himself be the gentlest of the gentle.

196   "Youngest he is then and gentlest, and also flowing of form. He cannot be rigid or stiff, else he could never enwrap in all ways, slipping in and out through every soul unheeded. His flowing and well-proportioned form is evidenced by his gracefulness, a quality universally granted, since eternal strife persists between awkwardness and Love.

b   "His habit of inhabiting flowers signals the god's fair complexion. He lights not in a soul, a body, or anything bloomless or faded, but in a fragrant and flowering place he settles to stay.

   "As for his beauty, that must suffice, though much has been left unsaid. I must now pass on to his virtues. Chiefest of these is justice: Love, in his dealings with gods and men, neither wrongs nor is wronged in return. Passive, he's not

c   passive by force—force may never touch Love—and active, all actively serve Love by consent, and what consenting parties consentingly do—that, says our law, the 'state's sovereign,'[29] is just.

   "Besides being just, Love is aboundingly temperate. Temperance admittedly means mastery of desires and pleasures, than which none is stronger than Love. If stronger, the others, weaker, are mastered by Love; if mastered, Love must master, perforce, all desires and pleasures and so be immoderately temperate.

   "Love has such courage as 'not even Ares can withstand.'[30]

d   For Ares possesses not Love, but Love Ares—love of

[28] The quotation is from *Iliad* 19.92-93.

[29] Quoted from Alcidamas, a pupil of Gorgias.

[30] From the *Thyestes*, a lost play by Sophocles. Ares is the god of war, in the *Odyssey* the lover of Aphrodite.

Aphrodite, so the story goes—and the possessor is more powerful than the possessed. And he who overpowers the most courageous god must be most courageous of all.

"I've spoken of Love's justice, temperance, and courage; his wisdom remains. I shall repair this liability to the best of my ability. First, to honor my craft as Eryximachus did his, Love is so wise a poet as to make poets of others. Whoever e Love touches turns poet, 'be he ever so museless before.'[31] This may pass as proof that Love is a great poet in all production pertaining to the Muse. For what one neither knows nor possesses can be neither given nor taught to another. Touching the creation of all living creatures, who would contest it's the wisdom of Love which causes the birth 197 and the growth of all living things? In the practice of crafts we agree that the man who has this god for a teacher will turn out brilliant and famous, but who the god touches not shall be dark and obscure. Apollo under the guidance of Love invented archery, prophecy, therapy; thus even he must be a disciple of Love. So in music the Muses, Hephaestus in b smithing, Athena in weaving, and Zeus in the 'steering of gods and men.' Hence the affairs of the gods were arranged after Love had been born—love of beauty, it's clear, since Love does not pair with the ugly. Before that, as I said at the start, many are the horrors said to have happened amongst them, under Necessity's rule. But since this god came to be, love of beauty has engendered all manner of good among gods and men.

"Thus, Phaedrus, I hold that Love is first fairest and best, c then the cause of like effects in others. I'm moved to speak verse and proclaim it is he who makes

> Peace among mortals, the hushed calm on the deep,
> stillness of winds, and in sorrow sweet sleep.[32]

Love brings us to brotherhood, flings us from otherhood, all d unions uniting like this, joining us one to the other, leading our sacrifices, dances, and feasts. All mildness providing, all wildness deriding, toward benevolence beneficent, toward malevolence maleficent, cheerful and good. To the wise he appears, all gods he endears. By the unfortunate he is pursued, the fortunate by him are imbued. Father of delicacy,

---

[31] An allusion to a line from the *Stheneboea*, a lost play of Euripides.
[32] An echo of *Odyssey* 5.391.

luxury, effeminacy, the Graces, desire, longing, and need.
For the good he's concerned, all evil he's spurned. In longing
e   and pain, in speaking and strain, our pilot, companion, best
savior, and friend; brightest adornment of gods and of men,
our fairest leader and best, whom all ought to follow exalting
in fair-sounding song, taking part in that hymn by which he
bewitches the mind of gods and of men.

"That is my speech, Phaedrus, dedicated to the god and
partaking, in so far as I could make it, equally of playfulness
and restrained seriousness."

198   When Agathon had finished, Aristodemus said they all
cheered wildly because the young man's speech had been so
appropriate to both himself and the god.

Socrates looked at Eryximachus: "Son of Acumenus," he
said, "do you still feel I felt a futile fear before, or was I a
prophet when I said Agathon would give an amazing speech
and I'd be at a loss for words?"

"I think you prophesied one thing truly: that Agathon
would make a fine speech. As for your being at a loss—I doubt
it," replied Eryximachus (said Aristodemus).

b   "My friend," said Socrates, "how could anyone not be at a
loss if he had to follow such a fair and many-sided speech as
that? Perhaps the earlier parts weren't so amazing, but that
ending! Who could have listened to that gorgeous diction and
phrasing without being smitten? When I reflected that I
wouldn't be able to come anywhere near such gorgeousness, I
was tempted to sneak away for shame, but there was no place
c   to go. It reminded me so much of Gorgias[33] that I felt like the
man in Homer: I was afraid at the end that Agathon would
throw the Gorgon's head of Gorgias, gorged with garrulity,
into my speech and turn me to stone with speechlessness. I
realized that it had been idiotic of me to agree to take a turn at
d   praising Love and to claim I was an expert when it turns out
that I don't even know how to make a eulogy. In my stupidity,
you see, I thought all you had to do was tell the truth about
the subject and, once that had been established, select the
most beautiful facts and arrange them as fittingly as possible.

[33] **The most famous** sophist and orator of the time. His style,
characterized by short, balanced clauses, jingles, and other ear
ticklers, is parodied in the ending of Agathon's speech. The pun on
the Gorgon below refers to the monster whose look turned men to
stone, *Odyssey* 11.634-35.

I was actually quite smug about my ability to make a good speech because I thought I knew the right way to do it.

"Now it turns out that that isn't the right way at all. The right way, it seems, is to give your subject the most beautiful   e
attributes you can think of, whether it has them or not. If they're false, that doesn't make any difference. It seems the proposal was not to eulogize Love, but to appear to. I assume that's why you exploited every conceivable argument to attribute to Love, saying he is so and so and the cause of such   199
and such: to make him appear as good and as beautiful as possible to people who don't know him—hardly to people who do!—and to make your speeches beautiful and grand.

"But I don't understand that method of making a eulogy, and it was out of ignorance that I agreed to make one. 'My tongue, not my heart, made the promise,'[34] and so I must break it. I won't give a eulogy like that—I couldn't do it. But I am willing to tell the truth, if you'd like, in my own way—not   b
in competition with your speeches, because that would make me look like a fool. So, Phaedrus, see if you can use a plain speech that tells the truth about Love, presented only with such diction and phrasing as occurs to me as I speak."

Phaedrus and the others, Aristodemus said, told Socrates to go ahead and speak in any way he thought proper.

"Now, Phaedrus," Socrates said, "please let me ask Agathon a few little questions so I can start speaking from a point we've agreed on."

"Go ahead," said Phaedrus. Then, said Aristodemus,   c
Socrates began something like this:

"Agathon, my friend, I thought you opened your speech very well when you said we should show first what Love is like and then his functions. I really liked that opening. Now, since you did such a marvelous job of describing his other qualities, tell me about this one too: Is Love the love *of*   d
something or not? By that I don't mean is he the love of a mother, for instance, or of a father—that would be a ridiculous question.[35] But if I asked, 'Is a father the father *of* someone or not?' I suppose if you wanted to give the right

---

[34] **Euripides,** *Hippolytus* 612. This notorious line, parodied by Aristophanes in his comedies, seemed to sanction perjury as long as you had "your finger crossed."
[35] *Eros* is passionate, sexual love; therefore the question is ridiculous when applied to a parent.

answer, you'd say he's the father of a son or a daughter. Isn't that true?"

"Of course," said Agathon.

"The same for a mother?"

Agathon agreed, said Aristodemus.

e "All right," said Socrates, "answer a few more questions so you'll see what I'm after. Suppose I asked: 'What about brother? Does that in itself imply a brother *of* someone?'"

Agathon said it did, said Aristodemus.

"Of a brother or sister, right?"

Agathon agreed, he said.

"Now try to answer my original question: Is Love the love *of* something or not?"

"He certainly is."

200 "Remember that answer," said Socrates, "—and also what you said the object of Love is. Now tell me, does Love *desire* what he's the love of or not?"

"Certainly," he said.

"Does he *possess* what he desires and loves and still desire and love it, or not?"

"Probably not."

"Probably or necessarily? To me it seems astonishingly

b clear, Agathon, that desire necessarily lacks what it desires and that without lack there can be no desire. How about you?"

"It seems necessary to me too."

"Well said, Agathon. Would someone tall desire to be tall, or someone strong to be strong?"

"That's impossible from what we've agreed on."

"Because he wouldn't lack the qualities he has."

"Right," replied Agathon (said Aristodemus).

"If someone strong wished to be strong, or someone fast to be fast, or someone healthy to be healthy—I'm harping on

c this so we won't be misled, because a person might think that someone who had these qualities could also desire them. But if you think about it, Agathon, a person must already possess each quality he has whether he wants to or not. And who would desire something like that? So if a man were to say: 'I'm healthy and I also wish to be healthy, I'm rich and I want to be rich, and I desire precisely the things that I have,' we'd reply,

d 'My friend, you already have health, wealth, and strength, so what you must want is to continue to possess them in the future, since for the present you already have them whether you want them or not. So when you say you desire what you already have, don't you really mean, "I wish to possess in the future the things I have right now"?'—wouldn't he agree that this is so?"

"Yes," said Agathon.

"Then that means he loves what is not yet possessed or available: the preservation and continuance of present things into the future."

"Indeed."   e

"So our friend and everyone else who desires, desires what is not present or available; and the objects of love and desire are things lacking, not part of oneself, and not possessed."

"True."

"Let's sum up our conclusions then: Love is first the love *of* things, then of things he now lacks. Isn't that so?"

"Yes."   201

"Now recall what you said in your speech is the object of Love. If you like, I'll recall it for you. I believe you said something like this: The affairs of the gods were arranged through love of beauty; there can be no love of the ugly. Didn't you say something like that?"

"Yes," said Agathon.

"And a most suitable speech it was too. But if that's true, can Love be anything except the love of beauty?"

"No."

"Didn't we agree that he lacks what he loves and doesn't   b
have it?"

"Yes."

"So Love must lack beauty and not have it."

"That follows."

"Very interesting. Do you really maintain that something which lacks beauty and never has it is beautiful?"

"No."

"Then do you still say that Love is beautiful?"

And Agathon said: "I'm afraid I didn't know what I was talking about when I said that."

"But your speech was so beautiful, Agathon. Now one   c
more question: Do you think that whatever is beautiful is also good?"

"Yes, I do," Aristodemus said Agathon replied.

"Therefore if Love lacks beautiful things, and if beautiful things are good, then Love must also lack good things."

"Have it your way, Socrates. I can't contradict you."

"It must be the truth you can't contradict, beloved

Agathon," said Socrates—"you could contradict Socrates easily."

SPEECH OF SOCRATES

d   "I'll leave you alone now, Agathon. The speech I'm about to give is one that I once heard from a Mantinean[36] lady named Diotima, who was very wise in many ways—once when the Athenians were sacrificing to avert the plague she postponed it for ten years—and she taught me all about Love. It is her speech, then, that I shall relate as well as I can all by myself, starting from the points Agathon and I agreed on.

"Agathon, you were right to say that we should expound
e   first what Love is and is like, and then his functions. And the easiest way for me to do that, I think, is to go through the same questions and answers the lady once went through with me. In different words I said much the same thing to her as Agathon said to me just now: that Love is a great god whose object is beauty. And she refuted me with the arguments I just used, pointing out that by my own reasoning Love was neither beautiful nor good.

'Do you mean to say he's ugly and bad?' I said.

'Hush!' she said. 'Do you think whatever isn't beautiful must necessarily be ugly?'

202   'Absolutely,' I said.

'And whoever isn't wise is ignorant? Or do you see that there's something between wisdom and ignorance?'

'What could that be?'

'Holding right opinions without being able to give reasons for them. You surely don't think something unreasoned is knowledge, do you? And stumbling onto reality isn't ignorance either. So I suppose this thing between knowledge and ignorance ought to be called "right opinion."'

'True,' I said.

b   'Then don't go forcing something not beautiful to be ugly or something not good to be bad. Just because you admit that Love is neither good nor beautiful, don't think he has to be ugly and bad—he's really between them.'

'But everyone says he's a great god.'

'Everyone ignorant, you mean? Or also people who know?'

'I mean everyone.'

[36] **Mantinea was** a town in the Peloponnese. Diotima is probably an invented character.

"She laughed and said: 'Socrates, how can everyone say he's a great god when there are people who say he's not even a   c god?'

'Who says that?' I asked.

'One,' she said, 'is you; another is me.'

'Diotima—how can you say that?'

'Easy. Look, do you call all gods beautiful and happy? Or would you dare to say there's one who isn't?'

'Heavens, no! I'd never say something like that.'

'By happy do you mean those who have good and beautiful things?'

'Certainly,' I said.

'But you just admitted that Love desires good and beautiful   d things precisely because he lacks them.'

'Yes, I did admit that.'

'Then how can he be a god if he lacks good and beautiful things?'

'He can't, I guess.'

'See? Even you don't believe that Love is a god.'

'Then what is he? A mortal?'

'No.'

'Well, what then?'

'Just as we said before: something between.'

'What can that be, Diotima?'

'A great spirit, Socrates. The whole spirit world, in fact, lies between the mortal and the divine.'   e

'What is its function?'

'To convey and interpret things from men to gods and from gods to men: requests and sacrifices from men, commands and returns for sacrifices from the gods. Being in the middle, the spirit world fills both worlds and binds the all to itself. Through the spirit world passes divination and the sacred sciences concerned with sacrifices, initiations, spells, all kinds of magic, and wizardry. Gods don't mingle with men;   203 all communication and intercourse between us, sleeping or awake, takes place through the spirit world. A man versed in such things is a spiritual man; one versed in anything else, whether a science or a trade, is merely a technician. There are a vast number and variety of spirits, Socrates, and one of them is Love.'

'Who are his mother and father?' I asked.

'That's a long story,' she said, 'but I'll tell it to you anyway.   b When Aphrodite was born, the gods held a feast. Among them was Resource, the son of Cunning. They had just finished a lavish meal when Poverty came begging at the door. Now, Resource had gotten drunk on the nectar—wine hadn't been invented yet—gone out into Zeus's garden, and fallen asleep in a stupor. Because of her resourcelessness, Poverty plotted to have a child by Resource, lay with him, and

c conceived Love. That's why Love became a servant and follower of Aphrodite: He was conceived at her birthday feast and is by nature a lover of beauty, and Aphrodite is very beautiful.

'As the son of Resource and Poverty, this is Love's plight: First, he's always a pauper, and far from being gentle and fair, as the crowd imagines, he's stiff and rough, shoeless and

d homeless, forever living in squalor and sleeping without a bed—outdoors on the ground, in streets, or on doorsteps. Having his mother's nature, he always cohabits with Need.

'Like his father, however, Love is a schemer after the beautiful and the good, an intrepid hunter full of courage, boldness, and endurance. He's forever hatching plots, and since he's resourceful and hungry for knowledge, he's a confirmed philosopher, a sorcerer and brewer of potions, and a skilled sophist. By nature he's neither mortal nor immortal,

e but when things go well for him, he'll come to life and flourish in a day, then die, then revive again. That's because of the resourcefulness he inherits from his father. But what his resourcefulness contrives always slips away from him, and he's never rich or poor for long because he's in the middle, between wisdom and ignorance.

204 'It's like this, you see. No god is a philosopher or desires to be wise. He *is* wise, and if there's anyone else who is wise, he's no philosopher either. So with ignorant people: They aren't philosophers and they don't desire wisdom. That's exactly why ignorance is so hard to deal with: An ignorant person is neither good nor intelligent, yet he's satisfied with himself because he can't desire what he doesn't think he lacks.'

'Then who are the philosophers,' I asked, 'if they're neither the wise nor the ignorant?'

b 'By now that should be obvious even to a child, Socrates. They're the ones in between, like Love. Wisdom, of course, is extremely beautiful, and since Love loves beauty, he must also love wisdom and be a philosopher, someone halfway between wisdom and ignorance. Love's heredity accounts for that also because his father was wise and resourceful, his mother unwise and resourceless.

'So much for the spirit's nature, dear Socrates. Your notion of Love was just a mistake, and not a very surprising one either. Judging by your statements, I'd say you mistook Love   c
to be Love's object rather than its loving force. I suppose that's why Love appeared so beautiful to you—love's object really is beautiful and delicate, blessed and perfect. But its loving force has an entirely different form, as I've explained.'

'Well, dear lady, you surely are a fine speaker. But if that's what Love is like, what use is he to man?'

'That's the next thing I'll have to try to teach you, Socrates.   d
You now know Love's nature and parentage, and his object is beauty, as you said. Now, what if someone asked us: "Why is Love of beauty, Socrates and Diotima?" or more clearly: "A lover loves beautiful things. Why?"'

'To get them,' I said.

'But that reply demands a further question: What does one gain by acquiring beautiful things?'

'I don't really seem to have an answer to that.'

'Well, suppose he exchanged goodness for beauty and said: e
"All right, Socrates, a lover loves good things. Why?"'

'To get them,' I said.

'And what does one gain by acquiring good things?'

'I do have an answer to that: happiness.'

'Because having good things is what makes happy people   205
happy, and we don't have to ask, "Why does a person want to be happy?" The answer seems to be final.'

'That's true,' I said.

'Do you think this want and this love are common to all men and everyone always wants to have good things?'

'I think so.'

'Then why don't we call them all lovers? Why some and not   b
others?'

'I'm surprised at that myself,' I said.

'It's not so surprising,' she said. 'You see, we abstract one form of love and give it the name of the whole. The other forms are called by different names.'"

'How do you mean?'

'Well, consider this: You know that creation is a broad thing. It's the sole cause of the emergence of anything from non-existence to existence, so that the production of things by   c
any craft is creation, and all craftsmen are creators.'

'True.'

'And yet you also know they aren't called creators, but have different names. Out of all creativity one part has been abstracted—the creation of music and poetry—and given the name of the whole. These are the only things called creation, and people with that kind of creativity are the only ones called creators.'

'True.'

d 'Well, the same with Love. Briefly put, all desire for happiness and good things is the prodigious, crafty love in us all. But people given to any other kind of love—such as love of money, sports, or knowledge—aren't called lovers or in love. Only those eagerly bent on pursuing one particular form of love are called lovers from the name of the whole.'

'I'll bet you're right,' I said.

e 'There's a story going around that love means searching for your own half. But I contend that love is neither of one's half nor of one's whole—unless, of course, it happened to be good—since a man would be willing to cut off his own hand or foot if he thought it was no good. So, my friend, I don't think we each cherish our own, unless you define the good as your own and the bad as the alien. Because what a man loves

206 is nothing other than the good. Or do you think differently?'

'No, by Zeus, I don't.'

'Well, can we simply say that men love the good?'

'Yes.'

'Wait a minute—shouldn't we add that they love to *possess* the good?'

'Yes, we should.'

'And not just to possess it, but to possess it forever?'

'Yes, we should add that too.'

'Love then, to define it succinctly, is the love of possessing the good forever.'

'That's perfectly true,' I said.

b 'Then what kind of pursuit of the good ought to be called love, and in what kind of activity is this eager intensity displayed? What is Love's function? Can you tell me?'

'If I could, Diotima, I wouldn't marvel at your wisdom and keep coming back to you to learn these very things.'

'Then I'll tell you: Love's function is reproduction in the beautiful, both in body and in soul.'

'Diotima, it would take prophecy to figure that out, and I don't have it.'

c 'But I have,' she said, 'a way to make this clear to you. You see, Socrates, all men are pregnant in both body and soul, and when we reach a certain age, our nature desires to give birth.

But birth isn't possible in the ugly, only in the beautiful. The *marrige.* intercourse of man and woman is procreation. This is a divine thing, for pregnancy and birth are what is deathless in creatures that die. But pregnancy and birth cannot take place in discord, and ugliness is discordant with the divine, d whereas beauty is concordant. Therefore Beauty is the goddess of birth. That's why when Pregnancy approaches beauty it feels cheerful and light-hearted; it relaxes and easily gives birth. Near ugliness, however, it frowns in pain, tenses and contracts in avoidance and revulsion, and doesn't give birth but painfully bears a withered, stillborn fetus. Hence the extreme excitement for beauty in someone who's e pregnant: it's a release from the terrible pangs of labor. For Love, Socrates, is not the love of beauty, as you think.'

'What is it then?'

'Love of reproduction and procreation in the beautiful.'

'Oh.'

'Absolutely,' she said. 'And why of procreation? Because that's as close as a mortal can come to perpetuity and 207 immortality. And if what we've said is true—that Love is the love of possessing the good *forever*—then we must desire immortality as well as the good. So Love is necessarily the love of immortality as well as of the good.'

"That's what Diotima used to teach me whenever she spoke about Love, and once she asked: 'Socrates, what do you suppose is the cause of all this love and desire? Or haven't you ever noticed the terrible state that birds and animals get into when they desire to reproduce? They fall sick with love, first b in regard to mating, then in regard to rearing their young. The weakest creatures will fight the strongest and even die for the sake of the young; they go hungry to feed them, and they make any sacrifice they must. You might think men acted this way out of calculation, but what can be the cause of such behavior in animals? Can you tell me?' c

"I said I didn't know.

"She replied: 'How on earth do you expect to become an expert on love if you can't even figure that out?'

'But Diotima, I just said that's exactly why I come to you, because I realize I need a teacher. So tell me the reason for this and for everything else about love.'

'Well, Socrates, if you really believe that the natural object of love is what we've so often said, don't be surprised at the conclusion, which is the same for animals as for men: It's the d nature of mortality to strive to exist forever and be immortal. And it can do so only through reproduction, so that a new, different individual always replaces the old. Even the individual, though each creature is said to be the same throughout its life—as a man, for example, is called the same man from youth to old age—nevertheless, he never has the same attributes. He is constantly being renewed, and old attributes are being destroyed. So with hair, flesh, bones, blood, the whole body and even the soul: A man's personality, habits, opinions, desires, pleasures, pains, fears—none stay the same, but new ones come into being as the old die away.

'Knowledge is even stranger: We're never the same even in what we know, not only because new knowledge comes into being and old knowledge passes away, but also because each bit of knowledge suffers the same thing that we do. What we call "practice," or "reviewing," exists because knowledge departs. Forgetting is the departure of knowledge; reviewing preserves knowledge by implanting a fresh, seemingly identical memory to replace a departing one. All mortal creatures are preserved the same way: not by remaining exactly the same forever like a god, but by each aging and departing individual always leaving behind a new, different one like himself. That's the device, Socrates, by which mortals partake of immortality, physically and otherwise. Immortals have their own way. So don't be surprised if every creature naturally respects its own offspring. It's for the sake of immortality that this love and eagerness accompanies them all.'

"I was amazed and said: 'Wise Diotima, is that really true?'

"Like an accomplished professor she replied: 'Irrefutably. Consider, if you will, human ambition as an illustration of my point. Unless you bear in mind what I've said, you'll be astounded at the irrationality of man's terrible erotic drive "to achieve fame and immortal renown for all future time." A man will risk greater dangers to win fame than to protect his children—he'll squander his wealth, endure hardships, even sacrifice his life. Do you think Alcestis would have died for Admetus, Achilles followed Patroclus into death, or your own king Codrus[37] willingly have died before his time to keep

[37] **An early king** of Athens. When Dorians were invading the city an oracle proclaimed that it would fall unless Codrus were killed. He

the throne for his family if they hadn't all believed that the memory we still have of their excellence would be immortal? Far from it, Socrates. I hold that all men do all things for the sake of immortal excellence and a glorious reputation like theirs, and the better the man, the more he does. For men love   e
immortality.

'Men pregnant in body go to women to express their love, hoping in that way to provide an immortal memory for themselves and happiness for all future time. But those pregnant in soul—there are some,' she said, 'more pregnant   209
in soul than in body, who conceive and give birth to the things of the mind, such as knowledge and excellence of the type that poets and inventors beget. By far the highest, most beautiful knowledge is called temperance and justice, which concern the administration of states and of private affairs.

'Such a young man, divine and since childhood pregnant in soul, desires to give birth when he comes of age and so goes   b
looking for beauty, since he cannot give birth in the ugly. Being pregnant, he cherishes beautiful bodies, and if he finds one whose soul is also beautiful, graceful, and noble, he rejoices in the combination and teems with resource in conversation about excellence and the qualities and activities   c
appropriate to the good man, and tries to teach this one.

'By attaching himself to a beautiful person and associating with him, he brings forth what he has carried so long, and present and absent he thinks of his friend and brings up his progeny with him, so that such lovers have a far stronger intimacy than ordinary parents because the children they share are more beautiful and also immortal. Everyone would prefer such offspring to human children and, looking at   d
Homer, Hesiod, and the other great poets, envy them the progeny they left behind, who have brought them an eternal memory and immortal fame. Or you may prefer children such as Lycurgus the lawgiver[38] left as saviors of Sparta and of practically all of Greece. At Athens, Solon is also honored for begetting the laws, as are countless other men elsewhere in   e

therefore slipped out in disguise, quarreled with some Dorian soldiers and got himself killed, thus saving the city and the throne for his descendants.

[38] **The traditional** founder of the Spartan constitution and framer of her laws. Solon, below, was an early lawgiver of Athens and a founder of her democracy.

Greece and in foreign countries, for causing beautiful works
to appear by giving birth to every kind of excellence. Some of
these men are honored like gods for their progeny, but no one
has ever been so honored for human children.

'So far, Socrates, the mysteries have been like a path which,
if followed correctly, leads to the final revelations. Perhaps
even you may be initiated this far. The rest, I'm afraid, will be
completely beyond you. Still, I'll reveal it—I won't lack
enthusiasm. So try to follow, if you can.

'A man who would approach love properly must begin as a
child and go to beautiful bodies and first, if his guide directs
him properly, love one beautiful body and in it bring forth
beautiful words and ideas; next he must notice that the beauty
of any one body is akin to that of all others, so that if one must
pursue beauty of form, it is absurd not to regard the beauty of
all bodies as one and the same. He has now become a lover of
all beautiful bodies; his violent excitement for one abates, and
he begins to despise it as petty. The next step is to honor
spiritual beauty above physical beauty, so that if he finds a
man good in soul without a blossoming body, he'll be
satisfied, love and care for him, and, by giving birth to the
kind of discussions that improve a young man, be forced to
observe the beauty of laws and customs, to see once again that
all beauty is kindred and so conclude that physical beauty is
only a paltry thing.

'After customs he must be led to knowledge and see its
beauty also, so that, having by now looked upon much
beauty, he'll no longer admire a particular manifestation of
it—fawning on an individual person, sweetheart, or custom
like a worthless, small-minded slave—but rather, absorbed in
the contemplation of a vast sea of beauty, give birth to
sublime words and sentiments in the unstinting practice of
philosophy until, having thus grown in power, he may
glimpse a unique knowledge—of a beauty I shall now
describe. So try to pay attention, as well as you possibly can.

'A man brought so far in love through the contemplation
of beautiful things viewed in their proper sequence will,
toward the end of his education, suddenly see something by
nature astonishingly beautiful. This, Socrates, is the goal of
all his previous struggles. First, it always *is*, and neither
comes into being and passes away nor increases and declines;
secondly, it is not beautiful in part, ugly in part, or now the
one, now the other; not beautiful compared to this, ugly

compared to that, nor yet beautiful here but ugly there, so as to appear beautiful to some but ugly to others. Its beauty does not give the illusion of being the beauty of a face, hands, or of anything the body partakes of, or of speech or a knowledge; nor is it *in* something else, as in an animal, the earth, the sky, or in any other thing. It is instead the beautiful itself as it b always *is*, one of a kind, by itself with itself; and all other beautiful things partake of that beautiful itself in such a way that their own coming to be and passing away neither increases it, diminishes it, nor affects it in any way.

'When, by proper boy love, a man ascends from things here and begins to glimpse the beautiful over there, he has almost reached the final goal. This is the proper way to go or be led to Love: to begin from beautiful things and ever climb, as on a c ladder, from one beautiful body to two and from two to all, from bodies to beautiful customs, from customs to beautiful knowledge, and from knowledge finally to reach that knowledge which is none other than the revelation of the beautiful itself, and so recognize at last what beauty really is.'

'That, dear Socrates,' said the Mantinean lady, 'is the time, d if ever there is one, when life is worth living—spent in contemplating the beautiful itself. If you should ever see that, Socrates, it won't seem to you to compare with the beauty of gold or of clothing or of boys and young men, whose beauty now so smites you—and others too—that you'd abstain from food and drink if you could and spend all your time watching the boys and consorting only with them. What then do you think would happen if a man could see pure beauty itself, clean and undefiled; if he caught a glimpse of it as it is, not e contaminated by human flesh or color or any other corruptible trash, but simple, divine beauty itself? Do you think life would be worthless then, when a man could look 212 over there with the proper faculty[39] and contemplate and consort with the beautiful? Don't you realize that it's only then, when he sees the beautiful itself with the faculty able to see it, that a man will bear not phantoms of excellence—since it's no phantom he clings to—but true excellence, because he clings to the truth? That in bearing and rearing true excellence this man, if any, will become god-beloved and immortal?'

[39] **I.e., reason or mind.** Cf. *Phaedrus* 247c (in a similar context): "Visible only to the soul's pilot, mind."

b   "That, Phaedrus and gentlemen, is what Diotima said, and I believe her. And because I believe her, I try to convince others that our human nature could not easily find a better partner than Love to help us attain that possession. Therefore I say that all men should honor Love, as I honor him and distinctively practice his ways, and I exhort others to do so, and now as always I glorify Love's power and courage with all the strength that I have.

c   "That is my speech, Phaedrus. Accept it, if you will, as a proper eulogy to Love. If not, then call it whatever you like."

When Socrates had finished, said Aristodemus, they all congratulated him except Aristophanes, who was trying to say something about the reference to his "story." Suddenly there was a terrific racket at the outside door. He said it sounded like revelers, and they could hear a flute girl playing. Agathon told the boys to go see who it was: "If it's some of our friends, let them in. If not, say the party is over and we're going to bed."

d

Moments later, said Aristodemus, they heard Alcibiades shouting drunkenly in the yard: "Where's Agathon? Take me to Agathon!" The flute girl and some others half-carried him in. There he stood in the doorway with a bushy wreath of violets and ivy on his head, and lots of ribbons. "Joy, gentlemen!" he cried. "Can I join the party roaring drunk, or should we just do what we came for—wreathe Agathon—and go? I couldn't come last night, you know, but I'm here now, with ribbons on my head to take from my head and put on the wisest and beautifullest head in town, if I may say so, like this. Will you laugh at me because I'm drunk? Well, I don't care—I know I'm telling the truth. So out with it: Can I join you on these terms? Will you drink with me or not?"

e

213

They all cheered, Aristodemus said, and told Alcibiades to come in and take a seat, and Agathon invited him in too. So in he came, led by his crew. He was undoing the ribbons as he entered and didn't notice Socrates because the ribbons were in front of his eyes. He sat down right next to Agathon, between him and Socrates, who had moved over when he saw him. He gave Agathon a hug and tied the ribbons on his head.

b

"Boys," said Agathon, "take off Alcibiades' shoes so he may recline as the third on this couch."

"Please do," said Alcibiades. "But who's the third?" As he spoke he turned around and saw Socrates. Up he leapt, exclaiming, "Heracles! What's this? Socrates! What are you

doing here? You were lurking here to ambush me, popping   c
up as usual where I least expected you. Why are *you* here? And
why are you *here*, next to Agathon? You never sit by
Aristophanes or some other clown, do you? Oh no, leave it to
you to finagle a seat next to the handsomest man in the
house!"

"Please protect me, Agathon," said Socrates. "This
fellow's love's no trifling matter. From the moment I first fell
in love with him I haven't been able to even look at a   d
handsome man without him flying into a jealous rage. He
makes a dreadful scene and insults me and can hardly keep his
hands off me. So see that he doesn't do anything now; reconcile us, and if he starts to get violent, protect me—I'm terrified
of his insane devotion."

"There's no reconciliation between you and me, Socrates,"
said Alcibiades. "I'll get even with you later. Now give me
some of those ribbons, Agathon. I'm going to wreathe this   e
amazing head too, so he can't say I wreathed you but not him,
even though he beats everyone at words all the time, and not
just the day before yesterday like you." With that he took
some of the ribbons and wreathed Socrates, then leaned back
again.

Aristodemus said Alcibiades settled down and said:
"Gentlemen, you look sober to me. That's no way to be—you
should drink! That was our agreement when you let me in. So
as master of ceremonies I choose—myself, till you catch up.
Agathon, have them bring me something big to drink out
of—no, never mind. Boy, bring me that wine cooler over
there!" (He saw that it held almost half a gallon.) He had it   214
filled, drained it, then told the boy to fill it again for Socrates.
As it was being filled, he said: "These tricks don't get me
anywhere with Socrates, gentlemen. No matter how much
you tell him to drink, he drinks it and doesn't even get
drunk."

The cooler was refilled, and Socrates drained it. Then, said
Aristodemus, Eryximachus spoke up: "Alcibiades, is this any
way to carry on, simply drinking like parched travelers with   b
no singing or talking over our cups?"

"Eryximachus, best son of the best and soberest father—
joy!"

"Joy," said Eryximachus. "How shall we do it?"

"However you say. We have to listen to you because 'One
doctor is worth a host of others.'⁴⁰ So give us your
prescription."

⁴⁰ The quotation is from *Iliad* 11.514.

"All right, here it is. Before you came, we resolved that we each would give a speech from left to right—as beautiful as we could make them—in praise of Love. The rest of us have spoken. Now since you've taken a drink but given no speech, it's only fair for you to give one too. Then set Socrates any topic you choose; he may do the same for the man on his left, and so on."

"Oh, that's beautiful, Eryximachus—to make a drunk man compete with sober ones so he doesn't have a chance. You don't believe Socrates, do you? Everything's just the opposite of what he says—if I tried to praise anyone else, man or god, with him around he wouldn't keep his hands off me."

"Why don't you be quiet?" said Socrates.

"No, by Poseidon—not another word about it. I won't praise anyone else as long as you're here."

"Well, go ahead then and praise Socrates if you wish."

"Do you mean it, Eryximachus? Can I attack him right here and get even with him in front of you all?"

"Hold on!" cried Socrates. "What have you got up your sleeve? Are you planning to praise me to make me look ridiculous, or what?"

"I'm planning to tell the truth," said Alcibiades. "Is that all right with you?"

"Of course," Socrates replied (said Aristodemus). "I'll encourage you to do that."

"All right then," Alcibiades said. "Let's do it like this. If I say anything that isn't true, break right in and call me a liar. Because I won't tell a lie on purpose. But don't be surprised if I get my story mixed up. Someone in my condition can hardly be resourceful enough to list your peculiarities in logical order."

SPEECH OF ALCIBIADES

"Gentlemen, I shall try to praise Socrates in similes. He'll probably think I'm doing it to make him look ridiculous, but my purpose is truth, not ridicule. I claim that Socrates is just like those carved Silenuses[41] you see standing in wood carvers' shops holding flutes and shepherd's pipes. They're hollow,

[41] **Bestial spirits** of the woods who spent their lives in lechery and debauchery. They are portrayed on vases as bald, bearded old men with flat faces, pug noses, and enormous erections. They sometimes have horses' ears and often chase nymphs. But they also have great wisdom, and Silenus (singular) was the teacher of the god Dionysus, sort of a mythological Falstaff. Socrates is often likened to Silenus for

and when you open them, you find little statues of the gods inside. I also claim he's like the satyr Marsyas. Even you will hardly deny that you *look* like a satyr, Socrates. But you're like them in other ways too. You're insolent. Isn't that so?—if you try to deny it, I'll produce witnesses. But you don't play the flute, you say? Ah, you do something much more amazing. Marsyas used instruments to bewitch men with the   c
magic of his mouth. Even today when his tunes are played—I call the tunes Olympus[42] played Marsyas's because he was his teacher—his tunes, whether played by an expert or some cheap flute girl, are the only ones that can make men possessed and show who's divine enough to be initiated into the sacred mysteries. But you beat Marsyas, Socrates; you do the same thing with the naked voice alone, unaided by instruments. The most eloquent speakers on the most   d
interesting topics leave us young fellows cold. But when we hear your discussions—either in person or second-hand—even if the speaker's not worth a damn—all of us, men, women, and children, are stricken and possessed.

"Gentlemen, if I wasn't afraid of sounding drunk, I'd take an oath and confess what I've suffered, and still do suffer, whenever this one speaks. Whenever I hear him, my heart   e
jumps higher than a Corybant,[43] tears stream down my cheeks, and I see that hordes of others suffer the same thing. When I used to listen to Pericles or other great speakers, I'd say to myself, 'This is a great speaker.' But I never went through anything like this: My soul didn't riot and accuse me of being a slave. But old Marsyas here has often gotten me into such a state that I felt life wasn't worth living if I kept on as I   216
am. You can't say that's a lie either, Socrates. Why, even now if I cared to lend him my ear I know I'd never hold out—I'd still suffer the same thing. He forces me to admit that even though I'm lacking myself, I still neglect my own self and try to run the government. So I have to hold my ears and run away from him like Odysseus from the Sirens[44]—else I'd sit

both his ugliness and wisdom, and his portraits show a great similarity to pictures of Silenuses. Satyrs were similar to Silenuses. Marsyas was supposed to have invented the flute. He challenged Apollo to a flute-playing contest, lost, and for his insolence was skinned alive.

[42] A Phrygian musician.

[43] **Corybants** were wild religious celebrants who, like dervishes, danced themselves into a state of mystical ecstasy and possession.

right down by him and never get away until I'd grown old and gray.

b   "And this one's made me suffer what no one would ever think I could: shame. He's the only one who's ever made me feel ashamed. I know I can't contradict him and say I shouldn't do what he says, but when I leave him, I'm seduced by my popularity with the crowd. So I sneak away and avoid him, and when I do see him, I'm ashamed for ignoring the

c   things we've agreed on. Sometimes I almost wish he were dead, but if that happened, I know I'd be more miserable than ever. I just don't know what to do about him.

"Those are the symptoms that I and many others have suffered from this satyr's piping. Now I'll show how else he's like a satyr and what amazing powers he has. Not one of you

d   knows him, but I'll expose him now that I've begun. You see Socrates as lusting after beautiful young men and always hanging around with them, starry-eyed and dazzled, ignorant of everything and not knowing a thing. Isn't that a regular satyr act? Damn right it is. But that's just an exterior he wraps around himself like a hollowed-out Silenus. Inside, gentlemen of the symposium, opened up, you can't imagine how full of temperance he is. He doesn't care if someone's handsome—it's inconceivable how he despises beauty—or

e   rich, or has any of the honors the crowd adores. I swear he thinks that's all worthless and we're nothing, and so he spends his life acting ignorant and playing games with people. But when he's serious and opened up—I'll bet no one's ever seen the statues inside him. But I saw them once, and they seemed to me so golden and divine, so amazing and

217   beautiful that—to put it bluntly—I had to do whatever Socrates said.

"I thought he was serious about my beauty, and I considered that a fantastic stroke of luck because all I'd have to do was favor him to learn everything he knew. You know how fantastically conceited I was about my beauty. So one day I sent my escort[45] home and managed to get alone with this one for the first time—I'd never been alone with him

b   before. Now, gentlemen, I must tell you the whole truth, so pay attention—and if I tell a lie, Socrates, you denounce me.

[44] **The scene referred to** is found in *Odyssey* 12.165-200.
[45] **Greek boys** normally did not go out unescorted; their escorts are the "slaves" that Pausanias referred to in 183c.

Well, I was *tête-à-tête* with him and thrilled, because I expected him to speak with me like a lover to his loved one. Nothing happened. He spent the day with me, talked with me the way he always did, and then went home.

"After that I invited him to train with me, to see if I could get anywhere that way. And he did train and even wrestle with me many times, with no one else around. What can I say? Nothing came of it.

"When that scheme failed, I decided to drop the subtle approach and make a direct attack and find out what was going on. So I invited him to dinner for two, like some lover plotting against his loved one. At first he turned me down, but finally he gave in. The first time he came, he ate and wanted to go home. I was ashamed and let him go. But I tried the same scheme again, and this time I kept him talking after dinner until far into the night. Then when he wanted to leave, I said it was too late and insisted that he stay. So he slept in the couch next to mine—the one he'd reclined on at dinner—and there was no one in the room but us.

"So far this has been a nice story that you could tell to anyone. But you'd never hear the rest if it wasn't for two things: first, the old saying—'wine and children tell the truth'; second, I think it'd clearly be wrong for someone making a eulogy to obscure such a brilliant and arrogant deed as this. Besides, I'm like a man suffering from snakebite. They say a man in that condition will only talk about it to others who've been bitten, because they're the only ones who'll understand and forgive him if his pain makes him talk and act wild. But I've been bitten by something more painful than a snake in the most sensitive spot—in the heart or soul or whatever you want to call it—by the words of philosophy, which are sharper than a snake's tooth when they sink in the soul of a decent young man, and they make him talk and act wild. Now here I see Phaedruses, Agathons, Eryximachuses, Pausaniases, Aristophaneses, Aristodemuses, and Socrates himself; you've all been stung by the madness and frenzy of philosophy, so you can hear the rest. You'll forgive what happened then and what's said now. But you slaves and anyone else who's rude and uninitiated—block your ears with heavy gates.

"Well, gentlemen, when the lights were out and the boys had left I decided not to beat around the bush but tell him exactly what I thought. So I nudged him and said:

'Socrates, are you asleep?'

'Not yet,' he said.

'Do you know what?'

'No, what?'

'I think you're the only man worthy of being my lover, but you seem shy about bringing it up. Here's how I feel about it: I think I'd be silly not to favor you in this or in anything else you might need, like property of mine or my friends. Nothing is more valuable to me than to become as good a man as I can, and I'm sure I'll never find a better partner to help me than you. And I'd feel much more ashamed around intelligent people if I didn't favor a man like you than I would with the ignorant mob if I did.'

"He didn't exactly lose control. He played dumb and answered in his usual way: 'You *are* a clever rascal, Alcibiades, if what you say is true, and I have the power to make you a better man. You must see some tremendous beauty in me totally different from your own good looks. If you're trying to get some of it by trading beauty for beauty, then you're planning to cheat me royally by exchanging counterfeit beauty for genuine, like Diomedes, who traded bronze armor for armor of gold.[46] But sly as you are, you'd better examine me closer to make sure I don't deceive you. The eye of the mind, you know, only begins to see sharply when the eyes in the head start to dim. And you're still a long way from that.'

'Well, now you know how I feel about it, anyhow. But you decide what you think is best for us both.'

'Well said,' he said. 'In the future we'll deliberate and do whatever we think best both in this and in everything else.'

"I'd shot my sharpest arrows in this skirmish, and I thought I'd wounded him. So without permitting the defendant another word, I got up, threw my coat over him (it was winter), climbed under his old cloak, flung my arms around this utterly divine and amazing man and slept with him the whole night long.[47] You can't say that's a lie either,

---

[46] An allusion to *Iliad* 6.234-36.

[47] Athenian legal language used a special pronoun to refer to one's adversary in court, which Alcibiades applies to Socrates. Here the reader expects Alcibiades to use a stock courtroom phrase: "this utterly vile and despicable scoundrel." Instead he says: "this utterly divine and amazing man," a contrary-to-expectation joke (like "once

Socrates. At that point the defendant treated me with such insolence, disdain, and contempt that he spurned my beauty—the thing I valued the most, gentlemen of the jury! (I call you that because you must be the judges of Socrates' arrogance.) By all the gods and goddesses, gentlemen, I swear that when I got up the next morning after having slept with Socrates, nothing more had happened than if I'd slept with d my father or an older brother.

"Can you imagine my state of mind after that, torn between humiliation at being rejected and admiration for this one's nature, temperance, and courage? He knew more and had more backbone than anyone I'd ever met, so I couldn't get angry and risk losing him, but I couldn't figure out a way to bind him to me either. I knew he'd turn down money as easy e as Ajax turned cold steel, and he'd dodged the one trap I thought could hold him. So I was baffled and ran around like a slave, enslaved to this one as no one's ever been enslaved before.

"All that happened before the Potidaean campaign,[48] where we were tentmates together. There Socrates showed he could endure hardships not only better than me but better than everyone in the whole army. When we'd be cut off somewhere and had to go hungry—which often happens on campaigns—no one came near him in endurance, and at 220 feasts no one enjoyed himself as much as this one without even drinking wine. But when we made him drink, he'd drink us all under the table. The most amazing thing is that no

seen, never—remembered"). The legal metaphor is made explicit below.

Alcibiades' formal charge against Socrates is *hubris*, which had a wide range of meaning in Greek: presumption, arrogance, violence, etc. It has been translated throughout as "insolence." Its basic idea is that of encroaching upon the rights and privileges of another, whether of a man, a god, or even a natural force (so in 188a-b Eryximachus can say that "insolent Love" causes disorder in the seasons and in the natural world). *Hubris* is not necessarily moral; it is a mere mechanical force, like a law of nature. It throws the world out of balance, but balance will be restored, mechanically, by another law of nature, *dike* ("justice"). In a narrower sense, *hubris* was a legal term for "assault and battery" or for contempt for another's person.
[48] **At the beginning** of the Peloponnesian war, 432-430 B.C. Potidaea is in the Chalcidice. The battle mentioned below (in d), where Alcibiades distinguished himself, occurred during the siege of Potidaea.

one's ever seen him drunk. I bet we'll soon have proof of that tonight.

"As for enduring cold—winters in Potidaea are awful—
b   Socrates was amazing. Once it was hideously cold; everything was frozen solid, and everyone either stayed inside, or if he had to go out, he bundled up fantastically and put on shoes and wrapped his feet in felt and sheepskin. But this one walked around in the same old cloak he always wore, and he waded barefoot through the ice easier than the others did with shoes on, and the soldiers began to suspect him of showing contempt for them.

c   "So much for that. But 'what a feat this mighty man dared and wrought'[49] on that campaign—and one worth hearing too. He fell into thought one morning trying to figure something out, and when it didn't come, he didn't give up but stood there searching for it. It got to be noon; people began to notice and shake their heads in amazement and say to each other: 'Socrates has been standing since morning, reflecting.'[50] Finally in the evening after supper some of the Ionians brought their beds outside, partly to sleep in the cool
d   breeze—it was summer then—and partly to watch Socrates to see if he'd stand there all night. And he did, till dawn. Then he said a prayer to the rising sun and walked away.

"And in battle—you've got to give him his due there too. When we fought the one where the generals awarded me the
e   medal for bravery, it was this one who saved me. I'd been wounded, but he didn't abandon me—he rescued both me and my armor. You know I told the generals to give the medal to you, Socrates—you can't criticize me there or say I lied. But they looked at my rank and wanted to give it to me, and you were even more enthusiastic than the generals and insisted that I get it instead of you.

"And you should have seen him the time the army was
221   retreating from Delium.[51] He was in the infantry, but I had a horse. The rest of our troops had been scattered, and this one was retreating with Laches. I happened to be nearby and saw

[49] **The quotation** is from *Odyssey* 4.242.
[50] **A funny-sounding** word in Attic. In the *Clouds* Aristophanes named Socrates' school the "Reflectory."
[51] **A fortification** in Boeotia, captured by the Athenians in 424 B.C. The Thebians attacked and defeated them as they were withdrawing their main army.

them, told them to buck up, and said I wouldn't desert them. This time I could watch Socrates better than at Potidaea—I was on a horse and less scared. The first thing I noticed was how much better Socrates kept his head than Laches did. Then I thought of your line from the *Clouds*, Aristophanes. b He walked there just like he does here in Athens, 'strutting along like a peacock, rolling his eyes around.'[52] He gave both friend and foe the same level look, and you could see from a distance that here was a man who'd defend himself if someone tried to touch him. That's why they both got away: the enemy almost never bother men like that; they go after the c ones that run away in panic.

"There are many other amazing things you could say in praise of Socrates, but the most amazing is his absolute uniqueness: He's not like anyone, living or dead. To Achilles you could compare Brasidas[53] and other generals, Pericles to orators like Nestor and Antenor, and everyone to somebody else. But this one's so strange, both himself and his speech, d that you could search and search and never find anyone like him, ancient or modern, unless of course you compared him to what I've compared him to—not to a man but to satyrs and Silenuses, both him and his discussions.

"Which brings up something I've completely overlooked: Socrates' discussions are also like those Silenuses that open up. The first time you hear them they sound completely e ridiculous. He wraps them up in words and phrases that remind you of the hide of some insolent old satyr. He talks about mules and saddles and blacksmiths and shoemakers and tanners, and he always seems to say the same things in the same way, so that anyone thoughtless or inexperienced would laugh himself sick. But once you see them open and 222 get inside them, you'll find that they are the only words that make any sense—they're divine and full of statues of excellence, and they concern everything a man ought to consider if he wants to become perfectly good.

"That, gentlemen, is my speech in praise of Socrates, mixed with my complaints about his insolence toward me. And I'm not the only one he's treated like that: He's also b deceived Charmides, Glaucon's son, Euthydemus, the son of

[52] *Clouds* 362.
[53] **A Spartan general.** Nestor (a Greek) and Antenor (a Trojan) were old and respected advisors in the *Iliad*.

Diocles, and many others, by pretending to be their lover and then turning out to be their loved one instead. So I warn you, Agathon, don't let this one deceive you. Learn from our experiences and beware, so you don't learn like the fool in the proverb—by suffering."

c   When Alcibiades had finished, Aristodemus said they all laughed at his frankness because he still seemed to be devoted to Socrates.

Socrates, he said, responded: "You seem sober to me, Alcibiades. Otherwise you'd never have been able to turn your speech back on itself so deftly and hide your real motive for saying everything you did, tucking it in like an afterthought at the very end as though your whole speech did not exist for

d the sole purpose of breaking up Agathon and me, because you think I should love only you and Agathon should be loved by only you. But you didn't fool us—we saw through your little satyr play.[54] Agathon, my dear, let's not let him have his way; let's fix it so no one can ever break us up."

"I think you're right, Socrates," Agathon replied (said

e Aristodemus). "I infer from where he's sitting that he's trying to come between us. But he won't get away with it; I'm coming over to sit by you."

"Right," said Socrates. "Come over here and sit on the other side of me."

"O Zeus!" cried Alcibiades. "Witness what this one makes me suffer. He thinks he has to beat me in everything. But if I can't get my way in this, you old fox, at least let Agathon sit between us."

"Impossible," said Socrates. "You praised me, and now I have to praise the man on my right. If Agathon were to sit on your right, he'd have to praise me before I could praise him.

223 No, let him go, you rascal, and don't be jealous if I praise the young man. The truth is that I want to very much."

"Oh!" said Agathon. "You can't keep me here, Alcibiades. I'm moving. There's nothing I'd like better than have Socrates praise me."

"It's the same old story," said Alcibiades. "With Socrates around no one else has a chance at the handsome young men. See how easily he found an excuse to get Agathon to sit by him."

[54] **A coarse burlesque** presented as the fourth play after a tragic trilogy.

Agathon got up to move. Suddenly a mob of revelers came   b
to the door, found it left open by someone in leaving, and
came in and sat down with the rest. The place was filled with
uproar and confusion and everyone was forced to guzzle wine
without order or restraint.

Aristodemus said that Eryximachus and Phaedrus and
some others got up and left, and he fell asleep and slept a long   c
time because the nights were long at that time of year. He
woke up toward morning when the roosters were already
crowing, and he saw that the others were either asleep or had
left and that only Agathon, Aristophanes, and Socrates were
awake and drinking wine from a large cup that they passed
from left to right. Socrates was having a discussion with
them. Aristodemus said he couldn't remember much of it—he   d
had missed the beginning and kept dozing off through the
rest—but the main point Socrates was trying to force them to
accept was that the writing of both tragedy and comedy is the
job of the same man, and a skilled tragedian also knows how
to write comedies. They were being forced to agree, though
they weren't following very well and kept nodding off, and
first Aristophanes fell asleep and then, when it was fully
light, Agathon fell asleep too.

Socrates, having put the two poets to sleep, got up and left,
and Aristodemus said he followed him, as was his habit. He
said Socrates went to the Lyceum and took a bath, spent the
day as he spent every other, and towards evening, he said,
went home to bed.

The Phaedo

ECHECRATES: Were you there in the prison, Phaedo,
when Socrates drank the poison,[1] or did you hear about it
from somebody else?
PHAEDO: I was there, Echecrates.
ECHECRATES: Then what did he say before he died? And
how did he die? I'd certainly like to find out. Hardly anyone
from Phlius goes to Athens any more, and no one from there
has come by for a long time. So we've really heard nothing   b
about it, except that he drank the poison and died.
PHAEDO: Didn't you even hear how his trial turned out?   58
ECHECRATES: Yes, and we were surprised that his
execution seemed to be so long after the trial. Why was that,
Phaedo?
PHAEDO: It was just an accident, Echecrates. You see, on
the day before the trial the Athenians had wreathed the stern
of the ship they send to Delos.
ECHECRATES: What ship is that?
PHAEDO: The Athenians say it's the one Theseus used to
bring the "seven youths and seven maidens" to Crete and then
saved both them and himself.[2] When he sailed, they say, they   b
made a vow to Apollo to send a sacred delegation to Delos
every year if the young people were spared. So every year
since, down to this very day, they send it to the god. And they
have a law that after the voyage begins, the city must be kept
pure and no one can be executed until the ship has reached
Delos and returned. Sometimes, if the winds go against them,

[1] **Hemlock**, the normal means of execution at Athens. The scene is set
in Phlius, a small town in the Peloponnese. It was a center of
Pythagorean philosophy and lay not far off the road from Athens to
Elis, Phaedo's home town.
[2] **Theseus** was a legendary king of Athens. King Minos of Crete had
imposed a tribute on Athens of "seven youths and seven maidens" to
be fed to the Minotaur every nine years. Theseus sailed to Crete, slew
the Minotaur, and freed the city from the tribute.

c   that can take quite a while. The mission officially begins when the priest of Apollo wreathes the stern of the ship. And that, as I said, happened on the day before the trial. That's why Socrates sat in jail so long between his trial and execution.

ECHECRATES: What about his death, Phaedo? What was said and done, and which of his friends were there? Or wouldn't the authorities let them in—did he die bereft of friends?

d   PHAEDO: Oh no, some were there—quite a few, in fact.

ECHECRATES: Please, Phaedo, tell us the whole thing as clearly as you can—if you have time, that is.

PHAEDO: Of course I have, and I'll try to recount it. I love to recall Socrates anyway, whether I'm speaking myself or listening to somebody else.

ECHECRATES: We're all as eager as you, Phaedo, so try to tell us everything as accurately as you can.

e   PHAEDO: Well, my own experiences on that day were amazing. I didn't feel pity as though I were present at the death of a beloved friend. The man seemed so happy, Echecrates, in both his manner and speech, and he died so nobly and fearlessly that I realized he was going to Hades by a divine dispensation and would, if anyone, also fare well over

59   there. So I didn't feel much pity, as you might expect of someone in the presence of sorrow, or pleasure either, at our usual philosophical discussions—it was simply a strange experience: an unusual combination of pleasure mixed with pain at the thought that he was soon to die. Everyone there felt much the same. Now we would laugh and sometimes we'd cry, and Apollodorus certainly—but I suppose you

b   know what he's like.[3]

ECHECRATES: Of course.

PHAEDO: Well, he certainly acted like that, and I was quite upset myself. So were the others.

ECHECRATES: Who all were there, Phaedo?

PHAEDO: Well, Apollodorus, of course. Others from Athens were Critobolus and his father Crito, Hermogenes, Epigenes, Aeschines, and Antisthenes. Ctesippus the Paeanian and Menexenus were there, and several other Athenians. I think Plato was sick.

ECHECRATES: Were there any foreigners?

---

[3] This **Apollodorus** is the narrator of the *Symposium*.

PHAEDO: Oh, yes. Simmias, Cebes, and Phaedondas from   c
Thebes, and Eucleides and Terpsion from Megara.
ECHECRATES: What about Aristippus and Cleombrotus?
PHAEDO: They weren't there. I heard they were in Aegina.
ECHECRATES: Was there anyone else?
PHAEDO: I think that was about it.
ECHECRATES: Then why not tell us about the
discussions?
PHAEDO: I'll try to tell it all from the beginning. The   d
others and I had gone to visit him every day, and we would
gather early in the morning at the court where he had been
tried because it lay close to the prison. We would wait around
there passing the time with each other until the prison
opened, which wasn't very early. Then we'd go in and spend
the rest of the day with Socrates. Well, that morning we had
gathered even earlier than usual because when we had left the   e
prison the evening before, we had heard that the ship from
Delos was in. So we agreed to meet at the usual place as early
as we could the next morning. When we got there, the
watchman who usually let us in came out and told us to wait
and not come in till he called. "The Eleven,"[4] he said, "are
releasing Socrates and giving orders that today he must die."
A little while later he returned and told us to come in. As we
entered, we found Socrates already released and his wife—you   60
know Xanthippe—sitting there with him holding their
child. When Xanthippe saw us, she broke out in laments and
started to carry on the way women do. "Oh, Socrates," she
cried, "this is the last time you'll talk with your friends."
Socrates looked at Crito and said: "Crito, have someone bring
her home."

Some of Crito's people led her out weeping and wailing.
Socrates sat up on the cot, began rubbing and bending his leg,   b
and said as he did: "How strange, gentlemen, is this thing
that people call pleasure! How strangely related to its
seeming opposite, pain: They refuse to occur in a man
together, yet if you pursue and capture the one, you're nearly
always forced to take the other too, as though they shared a
single head. If Aesop had noticed them, I think he'd have   c
composed a fable: how god, after attempting and failing to
reconcile the two as they fought, joined their heads into one,
so that wherever the one might appear, a little while later here

[4] **A board of** Athenian officials in charge of prisons and executions.

comes the other. That seems to be happening to me. My leg was hurting because of the bonds, and now pleasure shows up, tagging behind."

Cebes responded: "By Zeus, Socrates, it's a good thing you reminded me. Lots of people, including Evenus[5] just the other day, have been asking me about those poems you've composed by setting Aesop's fables and the Hymn to Apollo to music—what do you mean by composing now that you're here, when you never did it before? If you want me to have an answer for Evenus the next time he asks—and I know that he will—tell me what I should say."

"Why, the truth, Cebes: that I'm not trying to compete with him or his poems—I know that wouldn't be easy—but to check out the meaning of some dreams and to make amends in case this is the kind of music they've been directing me to compose. It's like this: The same vision has often come to me in my past life. It appears in different guises but always says the same thing: 'Socrates, make music and compose.' I used to think it was urging me to do what I was already doing, the way people cheer on runners, because I was already practicing philosophy, the greatest music. But ever since my trial the festival of the god has kept me from dying, and it seemed to me that the dream might be charging me to compose ordinary music and that I ought not to disobey, but to do it, because it's safest not to leave until I've made amends by composing poems in obedience to the dream. So first I composed one to the god whose festival this is. Then, considering that to be a poet one mustn't compose facts but stories and that I'm no storyteller, I took the fables of Aesop, which I had with me because I knew them by heart, and began turning them into poetry. Tell that to Evenus, Cebes. Bid him farewell, and say if he's sensible, he'll follow me as quick as he can. I'm leaving today, it seems. So the Athenians command.

"What a thing to pass on to Evenus, Socrates!" said Simmias. "I've dealt with him often, and from what I can see, he won't willingly follow your advice at all."

"What?" said Socrates. "Isn't Evenus a philosopher?"

"I think he is," said Simmias.

---

[5] A **sophist** from Paros who taught excellence for five minas (*Apology* 20b). "Music" has a wider range of meaning in Greek than in English. It covers "poetry" and even "education," so that Socrates can call philosophy "the greatest music."

"Then he'll be willing, like any decent philosopher, though he probably won't use force on himself. They say that's unlawful." As he spoke, he put his feet on the floor and sat like that for the rest of the discussion. 　　d

"What do you mean, a philosopher will be willing to follow someone who's dying, but won't use force on himself?" asked Cebes.

"You and Simmias have been with Philolaus, Cebes. Didn't you ever hear about this from him?"

"Nothing very certain or clear, Socrates."

"Well, I also speak from hearsay. But there's no reason not to tell what I've heard. It's probably fitting for someone about to move over there to speculate and tell tales about what he 　　e thinks the move will be like. What else should one do in the time before sundown?"

"Why in the world do they say it's unlawful to kill yourself, Socrates? I did hear that from Philolaus when he was staying at Thebes, and I've heard it from others too, but never anything definite."

"You must be eager, Cebes—maybe you'll hear it. Though 　　62 perhaps it will surprise you if, of all things, this alone is absolute: if, unlike everything else for man, it never turns out to be better for some people to die than to live; and it may also surprise you that it's impious for these people—who would be better off dead—to do themselves the favor, and they have to wait for some benefactor to do it for them."

Cebes chuckled softly. "Zeus sakes!" he said, slipping into his own dialect.

"It does seem illogical that way," said Socrates, "but it may 　　b still make some sense. The secret tale—that we men are kept in a kind of guardhouse and mustn't try to escape—strikes me as rather grand and hard to fathom. But that the gods have charge of us and we form one of their possessions—that seems right to me, Cebes. How about you?"

"It seems right to me, too," he said.

"Well, if one of your possessions tried to kill itself without 　　c any indication from you that you wanted it to, wouldn't you be angry and punish it if you could?"

"Of course."

"So in this way it doesn't seem so illogical not to try to kill yourself until a god sends some necessity, like the one now sent to me."

"That much seems reasonable," said Cebes. "But what you

d just said, that philosophers will be lightly willing to die, seems strange, Socrates, if what we just said is right and a god has charge of us as his possessions. It makes no sense for the brightest men not to resent leaving a service in which they're supervised by the best of existing things, the gods. They surely wouldn't believe they could take better care of themselves if set free. A thoughtless man might think he

e should run away from his master and therefore attempt a senseless escape without stopping to consider that one oughtn't to flee the good but stay with it. But a man with sense would probably desire always to be with his better. Put like that, Socrates, the reasonable course turns out to be the opposite of what you just said: It behooves a sensible man to resent dying, a senseless one to enjoy it."

Socrates seemed amused at Cebes' officiousness. He looked

63 at us and said: "Cebes is always tracking down some argument and doesn't like to believe what he's told."

"But Socrates," said Simmias, "for once it looks like he's got something. Why should wise men want to flee true masters—masters better than they—and lightly try to get rid of them? I think he's aiming his argument at you, because you take so lightly leaving both us and what you yourself admit are good masters, the gods."

b "Fair enough," said Socrates. "I take it you're saying that I should defend myself against this charge, as in court."

"Absolutely," said Simmias.

"All right, I'll try to make it more convincing to you than I did to the jury. If, Simmias and Cebes, I did not believe that I would come to other gods wise and good and to dead men better than these men here, then I'd be wrong not to resent death. As it is, you may be certain that I expect to come to

c good men—though I don't assert that very confidently. But that I'll find excellent masters in the gods—you can be sure that if I assert anything at all of the kind, it is that. That's why I don't grieve as much as I might, and I have good hope that something awaits the dead—something, as was said long ago, far better for good men than for bad."

"What, Socrates?" cried Simmias. "Do you intend to leave

d with that thought and not share it with us? I think that's a good to be shared and also your defense if you can make us believe it."

"I'll try," he said. "But first let's find out what Crito has obviously been wanting to tell us for some time."

"Just that the man who will give you the poison keeps telling me you shouldn't talk too much, Socrates. He says that speaking warms a person up, which counteracts the poison, and that sometimes people who talk a lot have to drink two or three times."

"Forget about him," said Socrates. "Just have him make enough for two or three times if it's needed."

"I was pretty sure you'd say that," said Crito, "but it was bothering me."

"Forget it," he said. "To you the jury, however, I now wish to present my argument: that it appears reasonable to me for a man who has spent his life truly in philosophy to face death with confidence and to have good hope that when he dies he'll collect the greatest rewards over there. How that may be, Simmias and Cebes, I shall now attempt to explain.

"Others, no doubt, fail to perceive that those who rightly engage in philosophy practice nothing but dying and death. If that is true, it would be rather odd if, when it came, they resented the very thing they had spent all their lives eagerly practicing."

Simmias laughed. "By Zeus, Socrates," he said, "you just made me laugh, though I wasn't much in the mood. But if most people—the Thebans especially—had heard that, I think they'd think it well said: Philosophers are really half-dead already, and others hardly fail to perceive that they deserve their condition."

"They'd be right too, Simmias, except for perceiving it. They don't see *how* true philosophers are half-dead and what kind of death they deserve and how they deserve it. But let's forget about them and discuss with each other. Do we think that death is something?"

"Of course," Simmias replied.

"Anything but the soul's being rid of the body? Isn't that death: The body becomes separated off by itself rid of the soul, and the soul by itself rid of the body? Is death anything else but that?"

"No, that's what it is."

"Now see if you share my opinion of this—I think it will help us to learn more about what we're after. Do you think a philosophical man would seriously concern himself with the so-called pleasures, like those of food and drink?"

"Not at all, Socrates."

"Of sex?"

"No."

"What about the other pleasures that cater to the body—having fine clothes and shoes and other bodily adornments—do you think he'll regard or disregard them, except as absolutely necessary?"

"Disregard them," he said, "if he's a true philosopher."

"Don't you think that generally speaking his business won't be with the body and he'll keep away from that as much as he can and be turned to the soul?"

"Yes."

"So it's in things like this that we first catch the philosopher trying to release his soul from its partnership with the body as much as he can, more than other people do."

"Apparently."

"And most people, Simmias, would probably think that a man who has nothing to do with that sort of thing doesn't deserve to live—if he doesn't care about pleasures that come through the body he's already flirting with death."

"That's absolutely true."

"How about in acquiring knowledge? Isn't the body a hindrance if you take it along as a partner in your search? Here's what I mean: Do sight and hearing present man with any sort of truth? Or don't even the poets constantly din into our ears that we see and hear nothing precisely? Yet if those two bodily sense yield nothing clear or precise, the others hardly will, because they're poorer than those. Or don't you agree?"

"Completely," he said.

"Then when does the soul seize truth?—when it attempts to examine something with the body it clearly gets deceived."

"True."

"Isn't it in reasoning and calculation, if anywhere, that something of reality becomes revealed to it?"

"Yes."

"And it reasons and calculates best when none of these things—sight, hearing, pleasure, or pain—annoys it; when it gets as alone by itself as it can, says goodbye to the body, and without clinging to it or being its partner, grasps for what *is*."[6]

"That's true."

---

[6] **The verb "to be"** is italicized when used in the sense of "exist" or "have true being," a use more common in Greek than in English.

"So here, too, doesn't the philosopher's soul especially disregard the body, flee from it, and seek to get alone by itself?"   d

"Apparently."

"How about this, Simmias? Do we say there's a justice itself?"

"We certainly do, by Zeus."

"And a beautiful itself and a good itself?"

"Of course."

"Have you ever seen any of them with your eyes?"

"Never," he said.

"Then have you grasped them with one of the other bodily senses? I'm referring to things like largeness, health, strength—in short, to the essence of all things, what each really is. Have you observed their abolute truth through the   e body, or is it like this: Whichever of us is most precisely prepared to think through every 'itself' that we examine will come closest to the knowing of it?"

"Of course."

"And the man who will gain the cleanest knowledge of them will be the one who goes after them each with thought itself, not adding sight to it or dragging any other senses into   66 his calculation, but using pure thought by itself to hunt down each pure thing that *is* by itself, as rid as can be of eyes, ears, and nearly his whole body, as a distraction that prevents the soul from acquiring knowledge and truth. Isn't he the one, Simmias, if any, that will hit being?"

"That's incredibly true, Socrates."

"And from all that," he said, "genuine philosophers are   b bound to get an opinion that will make them talk to each other something like this: 'I'll bet weaning ourselves from the body is a kind of a short cut that will bring us on to the track because as long as we're stuck with our bodies and our souls are mixed up with an evil like this, we'll never possess enough of what we desire, which we say is truth. The body and its necessary upkeep presents endless distractions, and if we fall   c prey to disease, that, too, hinders the hunt for what *is*. The body fills us with desires and passions, with fears and multifarious phantoms and whims—sheer nonsense that makes the old saying come true: Because of our bodies we can't even hear ourselves think. Then there are wars and quarrels and fights, brought on by nothing else but the body and its desires; all wars arise over money, and we're forced to own money because of the body, shackled to its service like   d

slaves. All this distracts us from philosophy, but the ultimate disaster is this: If the body does give us a moment's peace and we turn to the investigation of something, why, there in our searches it pops up again, spreading uproar and confusion all over the place, unnerving us so that we can't see the truth. So really, in our considered opinion, if we're ever to have clean knowledge of anything we must get rid of the body and
e   observe the things themselves with the soul itself. Then, it seems, we'll have our desire and what we say we love: knowledge—when we die, not while we live. So the argument indicates. If we're unable to acquire knowledge cleanly with the body, then we'll either never possess it at all or only after
67 we die. Then the soul itself will be by itself apart from the body; not before. And while living, we'll be closest to knowing, it seems, when we partner and traffic with the body the least—except as absolutely necessary—not infecting ourselves with its nature, but cleansing ourselves of it until god[7] himself sets us free. Then, clean and rid of the body's mindlessness, we'll be with our like and know through
b   ourselves all purity, which is probably truth. But for the clean to be grasped by the unclean is no doubt unlawful.' Something like that, I think, is what true lovers of learning are bound to conjecture and say to each other. Or don't you think so, Simmias?"

"More than anything, Socrates."

"If that's true, my companion," said Socrates, "then there's great hope for one going to where I'm going now that there, if anywhere, he'll sufficiently acquire what has kept us so busy in our past life, so that this moving away now enjoined upon
c   me ought to bring good hope to any man who believes his mind has been made purified and ready."

"Certainly," said Simmias.

"And doesn't purification turn out to be this, as was said in the tale long ago: separating the soul from the body as much as you can and habituating it to collect and gather itself up from every direction out of the body, itself by itself, and to live alone by itself to its fullest extent now and hereafter,
d   released as from bonds from the body?"

"Certainly," he said.

[7] **Plato** uses "god" and "the gods" interchangeably. There is nothing monotheistic about the singular; the use is generic, like "man" for "mankind."

"Isn't that called death—release and separation of the soul from the body?"

"Absolutely."

"And don't we say it's always and only those who rightly love wisdom that eagerly try to release it, that this is precisely the philosopher's study: release and separation of the soul from the body?"

"Apparently."

"Then, as I said at the start, wouldn't it be absurd for a man to make himself be and live as close to death as possible, and   e
then, when it comes, to resent it?"

"Completely absurd."

"Therefore, Simmias," he said, "true philosophers make a practice of dying, and they of all men have the least to fear from death. Look at it this way: If they are totally estranged from the body and desire to have their soul alone by itself, would it not be stupendous illogic if, when that happened, they should fear and resent it and not gladly go over there, where they have hope of encountering what they've loved all   68
their lives—knowledge—and of getting rid of an associate from which they're estranged? When so many men have willingly followed human sweethearts and wives and sons into Hades, drawn by the hope of seeing and being with their loved ones over there, would a true lover of knowledge with that very same hope—of meeting knowledge nowhere worth mentioning except in Hades—resent dying rather than go   b
over there gladly? We mustn't believe it, my friend—not if he's a true philosopher. His intense conviction will be that nowhere else will he meet knowledge cleanly. And if that is so, wouldn't it be stupendous illogic, as I just said, for him to fear death?"

"Stupendous, by Zeus."

"So whenever you see a man resenting his imminent death, isn't that proof enough that he's no lover of wisdom but a lover of the body? I suppose the same man will also love   c
money or honor, or both."

"Yes, it's just as you say."

"Doesn't so-called courage also especially apply to such philosophers, Simmias?"

"Absolutely," he said.

"And temperance—even defined as the many define it: not being flustered by the desires, but holding them in moderation and low regard—doesn't that apply only to them, who disregard the body and live a life of philosophy?"

d   "Necessarily."

"If you care to examine the courage and temperance of others, both will strike you as odd."

"Why, Socrates?"

"You know that all others regard death as one of the greatest of evils."

"They surely do," he said.

"And when the brave ones endure death, don't they do so out of fear of some still greater evil?"

"Indeed."

"So all but philosophers are brave out of fear and terror. Yet it's illogical for a man to be brave because of cowardice and terror."

e   "It surely is."

"What about the moderate ones? Don't they suffer the same thing—being temperate by a kind of self-indulgence? I know we say that's impossible, but still that's what their silly temperance turns out to be like. They desire certain pleasures and fear being deprived of them, and so they renounce some because they're mastered by others. They call being ruled by

69   pleasures 'self-indulgence,' yet it turns out that they master some pleasures because they themselves are mastered by others. So this resembles what I just said: They're somehow kept temperate through self-indulgence."

"It looks like it."

"O happy Simmias, I'm afraid that this isn't a proper exchange for excellence—trading pleasures for pleasures and pains for pains and fears for fears like coins, the smaller for larger—but that knowledge alone is the valid coinage for

b   which we must exchange all of those others: that courage, temperance, justice—all true excellence, in short—truly are what they are only in combination with knowledge, with or without the addition of pleasures and fears and all that; that all these pleasures and pains and fears, if exchanged for each other apart from knowledge, will produce merely a shadow drawing of excellence, truly slavelike and without anything healthy or true; that temperance, courage, and justice are actually a kind of purification from all that, and know-

c   ledge itself is a purification. It may be that those who established the initiations[8] among us weren't completely

[8] I.e., into the mystery religions (such as the Eleusinian Mysteries), which promised their initiates eternal bliss.

inept but were hinting all along that whoever gets to Hades uninitiated and imperfected will lie in mud, whereas the purified and initiated will live with gods. For what the initiators say is true: 'Many are initiated, but few are inspired.' These, in my opinion, are none other than proper philosophers, and in my life I've left nothing in my power undone but have been in every way eager to join them. Whether my eagerness has been properly placed and we've accomplished anything, we'll know clearly, god willing, when we get over there; quite soon, I imagine. That, Simmias and Cebes, is my defense—why it's reasonable that I don't take it hard or resent leaving you and these masters here— because I think I'll find masters and companions no less good over there. And if I've made my defense more convincing to you than I did to the Athenian jury, that is well.''

When Socrates had finished, Cebes replied: "I thought most of your speech was excellent, Socrates, but that part about the soul might overwhelm most people with doubt; they may fear that when the soul leaves the body, it perishes and is destroyed on the day a man dies and, released from the body, instantly flies away and scatters like wind or smoke and no longer exists anywhere. If it really exists somewhere, gathered up by itself and rid of those evils you just described, then, Socrates, there would be great and glorious hope that what you say is true. But precisely this point requires no little reassurance and proof: that the soul exists when a man dies and that it has some power and intelligence.''

"True, Cebes," said Socrates, "so what shall we do?—tell stories and try to find out whether this is likely to be true or not?''

"I'd like to hear your opinion of it," said Cebes.

"If anyone—even a comic poet[9]—were to hear us now," said Socrates, "I don't think he'd accuse me of being a windbag and discussing what doesn't concern me. So if this is what you think we ought to examine, then that's what we'll do.

"Let's begin by considering whether the souls of the departed exist in Hades or not. We all recall the old tale: that souls do exist there; they go there from here, then come back here to be born again from the dead. If that's true and the living are born again from the dead, then how can our souls help but exist over there? They could hardly be born again if

[9] **Perhaps** Aristophanes, who parodied Socrates in the *Clouds*, although Socrates was also parodied by other comic poets.

they didn't exist, and thus we'll adequately prove their existence if we can show that the living come from nowhere else but the dead. If not, we'll need some other argument."

"Certainly," said Cebes.

"Now don't judge only from men," he said. "You'll understand this more easily if we consider all creatures and plants and in short everything that has becoming, and see if this is how they become; in no other way than opposites from opposites—for those that have opposites, like the beautiful the ugly, the just the unjust, and so on, for countless others. If a thing has an opposite, let's decide whether it comes into being from anywhere else but its opposite, as when a thing becomes larger—doesn't it necessarily become larger from having first been smaller?"

"Yes."

"And if smaller, doesn't it later become smaller from having been larger before?"

"Indeed."

"And weaker from stronger and faster from slower?"

"Of course."

"And doesn't a thing become worse from having been better, and more just from having been less?"

"What else?"

"Do we have it well enough then? All things come about like that: opposites from opposites."

"Of course."

"Now, doesn't each of these pairs of opposites also have two becomings between them—from the one to the other, and from that back again to the first? Between a larger thing and a smaller lies increase and decline, and we call the first process 'increasing,' the second 'declining.'"

"Yes," he said.

"So with separating out and merging together, heating and cooling, and everything else. Even if we don't always have names for them, still in reality this is necessarily so: They take their becoming each from the other and each becomes the other again."

"Certainly," he said.

"Well, does life have an opposite, as wakefulness sleep?"

"Of course."

"What?"

"Death," said Cebes.

"If they're opposites, don't they come from each other, and

if they're a pair mustn't they have two becomings between them?"

"Absolutely."

"Now I'll tell you one of the teams I just mentioned," said Socrates,"—both it and its becomings, and you tell me the other. I'll say waking and sleep, and from sleep comes waking and from waking sleep, and their becomings are falling asleep and waking up. Have you got it well enough?"

"Certainly."

"All right, you do the same with life and death. Do you agree that being dead is the opposite of living?"

"Of course."

"And that they come from each other?"

"Yes."

"What comes from the living?"

"The dead."

"And from the dead?"

"Necessarily the living."

"So all that lives, Cebes, comes from the dead."

"Apparently."

"Then our souls exist in Hades."

"It seems so."

"And one of their two becomings seems clear enough. Dying is pretty obvious, isn't it?"

"Certainly."

"What shall we do now? Mustn't we supply the opposite becoming, or does nature limp here? Don't we have to provide some opposite to dying?"

"I suppose we do."

"What?"

"Coming back to life."

"Then if there's a coming back to life, wouldn't that be the becoming from the dead to the living?"

"Of course."

"So in this way too we agree that the living come from the dead no less than the dead from the living, and we said that this would be evidence enough that the souls of the dead exist somewhere, from where they're born again."

"That seems a necessary conclusion from what we've agreed on, Socrates."

"I don't think our agreements were wrong, Cebes. Look at it this way: If the one becoming didn't always receive its partner, didn't turn, as it were, in a circle but just went in a

straight line from the one opposite to the other without
making the turn and bending back to the first, don't you see
that everything would describe that same figure and suffer the
same thing and finally cease to become?"

"What do you mean?"

"Nothing difficult," he said. "If there were a falling asleep,
but no waking up were provided as a coming out of sleep, you
c   know that eventually everything would make Endymion[10]
look like an also-ran; he wouldn't even show, because
everything else would be in the same condition: asleep. Or if
everything merged and nothing separated out, we'd soon
have what Anaxagoras said: 'All things together.' In the same
way, dear Cebes, if all that took life were to die, and the dead
remained in that state and didn't revive, isn't it absolutely
necessary that finally everything would be dead and nothing
d   would live? If the living came from somewhere else and then
died, what device would there be to keep everything from
being squandered in death?"

"None whatsoever, Socrates," said Cebes. "I think you're
absolutely right."

"I think so too, Cebes—more than anything—and that we
weren't deceived in agreeing as we did. There really is a
returning to life, the living come from the dead, the souls of
e   the dead exist, and—"

"Yes," interrupted Cebes, "and if that argument you've
made so often is true, Socrates, that learning is nothing else
but recollection,[11] then we must necessarily have learned in
some former time what we recollect now. But that would be
73   impossible if our soul didn't exist somewhere before it was
born into this human form, so that this, too, makes it likely
that the soul is something immortal."

"What are the proofs for that, Cebes?" asked Simmias.
"You'll have to remind me—at the moment I don't recollect
very well."

"The most beautiful one," Cebes replied, "is that if you

---

[10] **A beautiful** youth beloved of the Moon. He was granted
immortality and eternal youth in the form of an unbroken sleep. The
quotation from Anaxagoras, below, refers to the state in which all
things were confounded together before Mind put them in their
proper order.

[11] **The argument** for learning as recollection is presented in *Meno*
80d-85b, where Socrates illustrates the theory by diagrams.

question people properly, they themselves will explain everything just as it is. That wouldn't be possible if they didn't have knowledge and a right explanation already in them. Also, if you show them diagrams or something, they'll give the clearest evidence that this is the case."   b

"If that doesn't convince you, Simmias," said Socrates, "look at it this way—you doubt, I presume, that what we call learning is recollection?"

"I don't doubt it," said Simmias. "I just lack the very thing we're discussing—recollection. What Cebes just tried to say, though, almost reminded me and made convinced—not that I wouldn't like to hear how you'd attempt to explain it."

"All right," he said. "I suppose we agree that if you   c remember something you must have known it before?"

"Certainly."

"And that knowledge is recollection when it comes about in a certain way? I mean like this: When someone sees, hears, or perceives something with some other sense and not only recognizes it, but also thinks of something else, which is known not by the same but by a different knowledge, can't we justly say he recollects the thing that he thought of?"   d

"What do you mean?"

"This: knowledge of a man is different from knowledge of a lyre."

"Of course."

"Yet you know that when lovers see a lyre or a cloak or anything else their sweethearts normally use, this is what happens to them: They recognize the lyre and at the same time apprehend the form of the boy it belongs to. That's recollection. In the same way, when a person sees Simmias, he may recollect Cebes—and so on for countless other things."

"Countless others," said Simmias.

"Then isn't that a kind of recollection, especially when it   e happens with things you've forgotten because you haven't thought about them for a long time?"

"Certainly."

"Well is it possible to look at a picture of a horse or a lyre and recall a man or at a picture of Simmias and recall Cebes?"

"Of course."

"And also at a picture of Simmias and recall Simmias himself?"

"Indeed."   74

"And from all that, doesn't it turn out that recollection may occur from either the like or the unlike?"

"Yes."

"But when a person recollects something from its like, doesn't he also necessarily notice whether or not the likeness falls in any way short of the thing it reminded him of?"

"Necessarily."

"Now see if this is so: I suppose we say there's an equal—I don't mean a stick to a stick or a stone to a stone or anything like that, but something besides all those, the equal itself. Shall we say there's something like that or not?"

b   "Absolutely, by Zeus—incredibly so."

"And do we know the equal itself that *is*?"

"Of course," said Simmias.

"Where do we get our knowledge of it? Isn't it from the things I just said: from seeing equal sticks and stones and so forth and then thinking of something else that *is*, which is different from them? Or doesn't it seem different to you? Don't equal sticks and stones sometimes appear equal and sometimes not, even though they stay the same?"

"Of course."

c   "Well, have the equals themselves ever appeared to you to be unequal or equality to be inequality?"

"Never, Socrates."

"Then these equal things aren't the same as the equal itself."

"Not at all, Socrates."

"But still it's from these equal things, different from that equal itself, that you conceived and acquired your knowledge of it."

"That's absolutely true."

"Because it's either like or unlike them."

"Of course."

"It makes no difference which. As long as you see one thing
d and it reminds you of another, like or unlike, that must be recollection."

"Necessarily."

"Now, do we experience something like this with sticks and the other equal things I just mentioned—do they appear to us to be as equal as the equal itself that *is*, or do they somehow fall short of it in equality?"

"They fall very short," he said.

"Then do we agree that when a person sees something and thinks 'the thing I'm looking at is trying to be like something

else that exists, but it's poorer and falls short of being exactly   e
like it,' mustn't he necessarily have had foreknowledge of the
thing he says this one is trying to resemble but falls short of?''

"Necessarily.''

"Well, didn't we just have an experience like that with
equal things and the equal itself?''

"Absolutely.''

"So we must necessarily have known the equal before the
time we first saw equal things and realized that they were all   75
striving to be like the equal, but fell short.''

"True.''

"And we surely agree that we realized this in no other way,
nor can it be otherwise realized, than by sight or touch or one
of the other senses. I regard them as all the same.''

"They are the same, Socrates, for the purposes of the
argument.''

"But from our senses we surely must realize that all the
equals that strike our senses strive for that equal itself but fall   b
short of it. Isn't that so?''

"Yes.''

"So before we began to see, hear, and use our other senses,
we must somewhere have acquired knowledge of what the
equal itself is, so that we could refer the equals that strike our
senses to it over there and see that they all aspire to be like that
but are inferior.''

"That necessarily follows from what we've agreed on,
Socrates.''

"Didn't we see, hear, and use our other senses as soon as we
were born, Simmias?''

"Of course.''

"And don't we say that we must have acquired knowledge   c
of equality before that?''

"Yes.''

"Then, it seems, we must have acquired it before we were
born.''

"It seems so.''

"Then if we acquired it before birth and had it with us
when we were born, didn't we know both before and
immediately upon being born not only the equal, the larger,
and the smaller, but everything else of the kind? Our
discussion isn't about the equal any more than about the
good itself, the beautiful itself, the just itself, the pious itself
and, in short, about everything that in our questions and   d

answers we stamp with the seal of the 'itself that *is*.' We must necessarily have acquired knowledge of all those before we were born.''

"True.''

"And if each time we acquired we didn't forget, we'd always be born knowing and always know all our lives. For knowing is nothing other than this: getting and keeping knowledge of something and not losing it. Or don't we call that forgetting, Simmias—dropping knowledge?''

e   "We certainly do, Socrates.''

"And if, I think, having acquired it before birth and lost it while being born, we later use our senses to reacquire that knowledge we had held once before, then wouldn't the thing we call learning properly be the reacquisition of our own knowledge? And wouldn't we be right in calling that 'recollection'?''

"Certainly.''

76   "We've shown it possible to perceive something with sight or hearing or one of the other senses and from it to think of something else that we had forgotten, because the thing approaches it either in similarity or dissimilarity. Thus we've a choice: Either we were all born knowing them and know all our lives, or else those who we say learn later on do nothing else but remember, and learning must be recollection.''

"That's certainly true, Socrates.''

"Which do you choose, Simmias? Were we born knowing,
b   or do we recollect later what we had known before?''

"I can't decide at the moment, Socrates.''

"Well, maybe you can decide this: Can a knowing man explain what he knows?''

"Necessarily, Socrates.''

"Do you think everyone can explain the things we've just been discussing?''

"I wish they could,'' said Simmias. "But I'm afraid that tommorow at this time, there won't be a person alive decently able to do that.''

c   "Then you don't think that everyone knows them, Simmias?''

"Not at all.''

"So they recollect what they had once learned?''

"Necessarily.''

"When did our souls get knowledge of them? Certainly not after we became human beings.''

"No."

"Before, then."

"Yes."

"So our souls existed apart from the body before they came to human form, Simmias, and they had intelligence."

"Unless, of course, we get that knowledge at the moment of birth—that time is still left, Socrates."

"All right, my friend—then when do we lose it? We just d agreed that we don't have it when we're born. Do we lose it at the same time that we get it, or can you suggest some other time?"

"No, Socrates. I guess I didn't realize that I was talking nonsense."

"Isn't this our position then, Simmias? If what we're constantly harping on really exists and there is a good and a beautiful and every such essence to which we refer all the e things that come from our senses, and if we compare these things to those as copies to originals, rediscovering what had once been our own, then just as they exist, so also our souls must have existed before we were born. If they don't exist, then our argument comes to nothing because either both they and our souls must have existed before we were born, or neither. Isn't that true?"

"Incredibly true, Socrates," said Simmias. "Both seem necessary to me, and I think our argument did well to take refuge in the double requirement that both our souls and 77 those essences you mentioned must have existed before we were born. Nothing appears more evident to me than that the good and the beautiful and all you just said exist absolutely. Our demonstration satisfies me."

"What about Cebes?" asked Socrates. "We have to convince him too."

"I think it will do," said Simmias, "even though he is the stubbornest fellow for doubting an argument. I believe he's fairly well convinced that our soul existed before we were born. But that it continues to exist after we die, Socrates— b even I doubt if that's been demonstrated, and what Cebes just gave as the popular opinion still stands: The soul may disperse at the moment of death, and that would be the end of its being. What's to prevent it from combining and coming into being from somewhere and existing before it enters a human body and then coming to an end and being destroyed when it leaves?"

c   "Well put, Simmias," said Cebes. "We seem to have half a
demonstration—that the soul existed before we were born—
and now, to make our demonstration complete, we must
prove that the soul will also exist after we die."

        "That's already been proved, Simmias and Cebes," said
Socrates, "—if you care to put this conclusion together with
the one we just reached—that everything living comes from
the dead. If the soul exists before birth, and if it necessarily
d   comes to life and is born from nowhere else but death and the
dead, then, since it must be born again, how can it help but
exist after we die? We've already proved what you demand.
Still, it seems to me that you and Simmias want to worry the
argument further, like children afraid that the wind might
scatter the soul and blow it away when it leaves the body,
e   especially if one happens to die not on a calm but a blustery
day."

        Cebes burst out laughing: "Try to persuade us like scared
children, Socrates. Actually it's probably not us but a child in
us that fears such things. So try to reassure him not to be
frightened by death like the bogeyman."

        "Yes," said Socrates, "we must sing him incantations every
day until we've charmed his fear away."

78   "Where will we find a good charm for that kind of thing
after you leave us, Socrates?"

        "Greece is wide, Cebes," he said, "and she probably has
some good men. There are also many barbarian countries.
You must hunt through them all for this charm, sparing
neither money nor toil, because you'll find nothing more
timely to spend them on. You must also search with each
other; you may not easily find anyone more able to do this
than you."

        "We'll do that," said Cebes. "But now let's return to where
b   we left off, if you'd be happy with that."

        "Of course. Why shouldn't I be happy?"

        "Fine," he said.

        "Well, shouldn't we ask ourselves what kind of a thing this
dispersion, and therefore the fear of its happening, pertains
to, and what kind of a thing it does not? Then we can examine
which kind is the soul and from that either fear or have
confidence for our own."

        "True," he said.

c   "Doesn't dividing up in the way it was composed pertain to
compounds and to naturally composite things? Only an

uncompounded thing, if anything, doesn't suffer that."

"That seems right to me," said Cebes.

"Isn't what's always the same in every respect most likely uncompounded, and what's never the same but different at different times most likely compounded?"

"I think so."

"Now let's return to the things we discussed earlier," he said. "Essence itself, whose being we account for in our   d
questions and answers—is that always the same in every respect, or always different? Does the equal itself, the beautiful itself, every itself that *is*, which is being, accept any change? Or does each of them that *is*, being one of a kind by itself, stay always in every way ever the same and never in any way accept the slightest change whatsoever?"

"They necessarily always stay the same in every respect, Socrates," said Cebes.

"What about the many beautiful things—men, horses, cloaks, and so on—and equal things, and all the other many   e
things that have the same names as those? Are these always the same, or, in direct opposition to those, are they practically never the same in any way with themselves or each other?"

"The latter," said Cebes, "—never the same."

"And can't you touch and see these, and perceive them with   79
the other senses, while those that stay always the same can never be caught with anything but the mind's reasoning because they're unseen and invisible?"

"That's absolutely true, Socrates."

"Then shall we posit two classes of existing things, the visible and the invisible?"

"Yes."

"And the invisible is always the same, the visible never?"

"Indeed."

"Now, don't we consist of body and soul?"   b

"Yes."

"Which class shall we say the body more closely resembles and is related to?"

"Obviously the visible."

"And the soul? is it visible?"

"Not to human eyes, at any rate."

"But surely we define this in reference to human nature—or do you think it's to some other?"

"No, that one."

"What about the soul then? Is it seen or unseen?"

"Unseen."

"Then it's invisible."

"Yes."

"So the soul is more like the invisible, the body more like the visible."

c   "An absolute necessity, Socrates."

"And haven't we said all along that when the soul uses the body to examine something, either by sight, hearing, or one of the other senses—using the body means examining with the senses—it gets dragged by the body to what's never the same and, clutching to such things, wanders in confusion and staggers as though it were drunk?"

"Of course."

d   "But when it examines alone by itself it goes over there to the pure, ever-existing, immortal, and selfsame, and, being related to that, always stays with it whenever it gets alone by itself and can do so, and, clutching to such things, desists from its wandering and remains always the same toward them in every respect. Don't we call such a condition of the soul 'knowledge'?"

"That's absolutely true, Socrates."

"Then from this and from what we said earlier, which class

e   do you think the soul most closely resembles and is related to, Cebes?"

"Pursuing it this way, Socrates, I think even the slowest learner would have to admit that the soul completely resembles what always stays the same rather than what does not."

"And the body?"

"The other."

"Now look at it this way: When body and soul are together,

80 nature directs the body to be ruled as a slave, the soul to rule as the master. So going by that, which do you think is more like the divine and which like the mortal? Or don't you think it's the nature of the divine to rule and to lead, of the mortal to be ruled and enslaved?"

"Yes, I do."

"Then which does the soul resemble?"

"Obviously, Socrates, the soul resembles the divine, the body the mortal."

"Now, Cebes, consider whether this is the conclusion of all

b   that we've said: The soul is most like the divine, immortal, intelligible, single-formed, indissoluble, and the ever selfsame in every respect; the body like the human, mortal, multiformed, unintelligent, dissoluble, and the never selfsame in any respect. Is that so, dear Cebes, or can we say something else?"

"No, that's so."

"Then mustn't rapid dissolution pertain to the body, absolute indissolubility—or something close to it—to the soul?"

"What else?"   c

"Now you'll notice that when a man dies, his visible part, the body, which also lies in the visible and which we call a corpse, to which pertain dissolution and collapse and being blown away, suffers none of these instantly but lasts a fairly long time, even if he dies in fair condition and in a fair season. And if the body is shriveled, or embalmed as in Egypt, it lasts an almost inconceivably long time, and parts of it—bones   d and sinews and so on—are practically immortal even if the body decays. Isn't that so?"

"Yes."

"Yet the soul, the invisible part, which goes to a place as noble, invisible and pure as itself, to 'unseen Hades'[12] and to the good and intelligent god—where, god willing, my soul soon must go—would a thing like that when released from the body be instantly wafted away and destroyed, as most people say? Far from it, dear Cebes and Simmias, but far   e rather so: If it departs pure, dragging with it nothing of the body because in life it never willingly partnered with it, but fled the body and gathered itself to itself as its constant practice—which is precisely right philosophy and the true practice of facing death lightly. Or isn't that what we mean by   81 'practicing death'?"

"Exactly."

"Then won't a soul in that condition go to its like, to the invisible, divine, immortal, and intelligent, where it redounds to it to be happy, freed from wandering and folly, from fears, cruel passions, and all other human evils and where, as is said of the initiated, it truly spends all future time with gods? Shall we say that, Cebes, or not?"

"Yes, by Zeus," Cebes replied.

"But if, I believe, it departs defiled and uncleansed of the   b body because it always consorted with it, loved it, catered to it,

[12] The name "Hades" (the god of the underworld) was popularly understood as meaning "unseen."

and was so fascinated by it and its desires and pleasures that it considered nothing else to be true but bodily things—things one can see and touch and eat and drink and make love to—and habitually hated, dreaded, and fled what is dark and invisible to the eye, but intelligible and tangible to
c   philosophy—do you think a soul in that condition will depart alone by itself and pure?"

"Not at all," he said.

"Because it's patched with corporality, which its intercourse with the body has made innate in it by long association and continual practice."

"Of course."

"And we must imagine corporality as weighty, earthy, heavy, and visible, so that such souls are weighed down and dragged back to the visible region by fear of Hades and the
d   invisible, and haunt their tombs and monuments where, they say, shadowy apparitions may sometimes be seen as phantoms cast by such souls, which didn't depart cleanly but cling to the visible and so can be seen."

"Most likely, Socrates."

"Likely indeed, Cebes. And they're souls not of good men but scoundrels, forced to wander and pay recompense for their previous evil habits. Thus they must wander until from
e   desire for their lingering corporality they're again imprisoned in a body. They assume, as you'd expect, dispositions like the habits they had practiced in life."

"What do you mean, Socrates?"

"Well, reckless gluttons and drunkards and insolent hoodlums, for instance, most likely become mules and
82 similar animals, don't you think?"

"It surely seems likely."

"And those who preferred injustice, tyranny, and rapine become species like wolves and hawks and falcons. Where else shall we say souls like that end up?"

"Nowhere, Socrates—that seems right."

"Then isn't it clear where the others will go, determined by their previous practices?"

"Very clear."

"So wouldn't the happiest of those, who go to the best place, be the ones who pursued the virtues of an ordinary
b   citizen—what they call temperance and justice—acquired by habit and practice without philosophy and reason?"

"How will they be the happiest?"

"They'll likely return to some gentle, civilized species like bees or wasps or ants, or even to the human race again, so that from them come moderate men."

"Most likely."

"But to go to the race of gods is unlawful for any who departs without having been completely purified in c philosophy. For this reason, dear Simmias and Cebes, proper philosophers abstain from all bodily desires and persistently refuse to give themselves up to them—not from fear of financial ruin or poverty, like the many lovers of money, or from fear of dishonor or disgrace, like men who love honor or power."

"No, that would hardly be fitting, Socrates."

"Not at all, by Zeus. Therefore, Cebes, those who care for d their souls and don't live for forming their bodies say farewell to the ones who don't know where they're going; they take a different path because they don't think they ought to act contrary to philosophy and its release and purification, but turn to it and follow wherever it leads."

"How, Socrates?"

"Like this: Lovers of learning know that philosophy takes up their soul literally imprisoned and stuck to the body, e wallowing in ignorance and forced to peer at reality through the body as though through a cage rather than directly, through itself; and philosophy sees the cage's cunning, that it consists of desire, so that the prisoner himself is the main accomplice in his own imprisonment—lovers of learning, 83 therefore, know that philosophy takes up their soul in that condition and gently reassures and tries to release it, points out that observation by eyes (as well as by ears and the rest of the senses) is filled with deceit, persuades the soul to draw away from the senses—except where absolutely necessary to use them—and urges it to collect and gather itself up alone by itself and to trust only itself and those entities themselves b which it discerns by itself; those which it observes by different means as being different in different things it must never regard as true: such things are perceptible and visible, but what it sees by itself are intelligible and invisible. Believing, therefore, that it ought not to oppose this release, the true philosopher's soul abstains from desires and pleasures and pains as much as it can, reflecting that when one feels intense pleasure, desire, or fear, one does not suffer such an evil from them as one might expect—sickness, or some loss because of c desire—but the greatest disaster of all, without even taking it into account."

"What is that, Socrates?" asked Cebes.

"That every person's soul, during the time that it feels intense pleasure or pain at something, is forced to consider that thing to be the most vivid and true, though it is not. These are mostly visible things, aren't they?"

"Of course."

d "Isn't it in such states that the soul is most tied down by the body?"

"How?"

"It's as if each pleasure and pain had a nail in it. They nail the soul to the body and make it bodylike, so that it imagines the truth to be whatever the body tells it. From sharing the same opinions and joys as the body, I think the soul is also forced to share the same habits and life and to turn into something that never gets to Hades pure, but always departs contaminated by the body so that it falls right back into

e another body, grows in it like a seed, and remains cut off from all intercourse with the divine, the pure, and the single-formed."

"That's absolutely true, Socrates," said Cebes.

"This is the reason, Cebes, that those justly called lovers of learning are moderate and brave; not for the reason most people think. Or do you think so?"

84 "Not at all, Socrates."

"No. The philosopher's soul will reason like this and think it ought not to release itself by philosophy and then, when released, surrender itself once more to pleasures and pains and tie itself down again, attempting an unfulfillable task, a sort of Penelope's web[13] in reverse, but secure tranquillity from pleasures and pains and, following reason and being always occupied with it, observe the divine, unconjectured,

b and true, and so live this life nourished by that and after death go to its related and like, rid of human evils. After being nurtured like that, Simmias and Cebes, it needn't fear that when leaving the body, it may be scattered and blown away by the wind and fly off and no longer exist anywhere."

c A long silence followed. Socrates appeared to be absorbed in the foregoing discussion, as were most of us. But Cebes and

[13] **Penelope** was courted by a pack of insolent suitors during the absence of her husband Odysseus. She promised to choose one of them as her husband after she had finished weaving a web. Every night she unwove what she had woven during the day.

Simmias were whispering together. Socrates looked at them and said: "I suppose our argument seems deficient to you? It certainly offers plenty of openings for counterholds and misgivings if you run through it thoroughly. So if you're examining something else, fine. But if you're baffled by something in this, don't hesitate to go back over it if you think you can improve on it somehow, or to take me along with you if you think I might be able to help you out of your straits."

Simmias replied: "I'll tell you the truth, Socrates. We've been baffled for some time now and have been urging each other to ask because we'd like to hear what you say, but we hesitate to bother you with something you may find unpleasant in your present misfortune."

Socrates laughed quietly. "Tush, Simmias!" he said. "I could hardly persuade others that I don't consider this a misfortune if I can't even convince you, and you're afraid that I'm less content now than I was in former days. You must think me a poorer prophet than the swans, who when they see that they must die sing more sweetly than ever before, for delight at going to the god whose servants they are. Men, because of their own fear of death, misrepresent them by saying their song is a sorrowful lament for death. They don't reflect that no bird sings when it suffers—not even the nightingale or swallow or hoopoe, whose songs they call laments. I think that neither they nor the swans sing for sorrow, but as prophet birds of Apollo that foresee the good things in Hades they sing for joy, greater on that day than on any other. I consider myself the swans' fellow slave, consecrated to the same god; to me the master has given prophecy no poorer than theirs, and I leave life no more despondent than they. Therefore you must ask and say whatever you wish for as long as the Athenian Eleven permit."

"Fine," said Simmias. "I'll tell you what baffles me, and then Cebes can say what he doesn't accept in the argument. It seems to me, Socrates—and to you also, perhaps—that to know anything certain about such things in this life is either impossible or exceedingly difficult, but to give up without completely testing the views on the subject and before you're totally exhausted from examining them on every side is the mark of a weakling. For we must accomplish one of the following: either learn the truth about this from someone else or find it out for ourselves or, if that's impossible, at least catch the best, most irrefutable human argument we can find,

d   and ride on it like a raft, sailing through life taking our chances on it, unless we can get safer, less dangerous passage on a securer vessel in the form of some divine explanation. So now I won't be embarrassed to speak, especially since you said we should, and then I won't have to blame myself later for not giving my opinion now. Because, Socrates, after examining our argument both with myself and with Cebes here, I've concluded that it isn't enough."

e   Socrates replied: "Perhaps, my companion, your conclusion is right. But tell how it seems insufficient."

"Like this, I think: One could make the same argument about a harmony and a lyre and its strings—that the harmony of a well-tuned lyre is something invisible, bodiless,

86   beautiful, and divine, whereas the lyre itself and its strings are corporeal, composite, earthy bodies akin to the mortal. Now if someone smashed a lyre or broke its strings and then used your argument to assert that the harmony still existed and wasn't destroyed because no device could enable the lyre with its broken strings, which are mortal, to continue to exist

b   when the harmony, which is related to and of like nature with the divine, is destroyed, the immortal before the mortal, but claimed instead that the harmony itself must still exist somewhere and that the wood and the strings will rot before the harmony suffers a thing—for surely, Socrates, you yourself, I think, must realize that we take the soul to be exactly that kind of a thing; that just as our bodies are strung and held together by the hot and cold, the wet and dry, and all that sort of thing, so our soul is a blending or harmony of

c   these very same things, when they're blended in proper measure—if, therefore, the soul is a kind of harmony, then clearly when our body's tuning is disturbed by disease or some other evil, the soul, though divine, must instantly vanish, like the harmonies of notes and of all crafted instruments, even though the remains of each body last a long

d   time, until they're burned or they rot. So see what we'd say to this argument, that the soul is a blending of the body's elements and is the first thing to perish in what we call death."

Socrates smiled and stared at us the way he often did. "Not a bad objection," he said. "Simmias is certainly no bungler at handling an argument. So if one of you is more resourceful

than I, why not answer? But perhaps before answering him
we should listen to Cebes, too, so we have time to plan our   e
reply. Then if what the two of them say seems to chime, we'll
concur; if not, we'll defend the argument. So come, Cebes—
tell us what bothers you so much."

"I will," said Cebes. "It seems to me that the argument is
still where it was and open to the same objection we made
before. I won't take back what I said about our soul existing   87
before it came to this form—I think that part was
demonstrated elegantly and, if the word isn't too fulsome,
amply. But that it continues to exist somewhere after we die
doesn't strike me as having been proved. Not that I agree with
Simmias about the soul being weaker and shorter-lived than
the body. I think it's far superior in all such respects. 'Then
why,' the argument might ask, 'do you still doubt, when you
see that a man's weaker part still exists after death? Don't you
think his longer-lived part is necessarily preserved during   b
that time?'

"Now examine my reply and see if it makes any sense. Like
Simmias, it seems that I too need a simile. It's as if an old
weaver had died and you used this argument to prove that the
man hadn't perished but was safe somewhere, and produced
as evidence the cloak he had worn and made, pointing out
that it was still safe and undestroyed; and then, if someone
disbelieved you, you would ask which lasts longer, a man or a   c
cloak in daily use, and upon receiving the answer, 'a man, by
far,' believe you had proved that the man was absolutely safe
and sound, since the shorter-lived thing hadn't perished. I
don't think that's valid, Simmias—I want you to examine
this too. Anyone would say that your argument was silly.
That weaver had made and worn out many such cloaks; he
outlived all of the others and died only before the last, and a   d
man is no poorer or weaker than a cloak for that.

"I think this simile illustrates the relation of the soul to the
body, and it would strike me as reasonable if someone used it
to show that the soul is a long-lived thing, the body a weak,
short-lived one. 'Each soul,' he would say, 'wears out many
bodies, especially if it lives a long time—for though the body
"flows"[14] and continually perishes while a man lives, still the

[14] **Apparently** an allusion to the saying of Heraclitus, "everything
flows." Heraclitus (ca. 500 B.C.) maintained that everything changes;
the only thing constant is change itself.

e   soul constantly reweaves the worn-out parts—and when the soul perishes it must necessarily be wearing its latest web and perish before that one only; and after the soul dies, then the body displays its natural weakness by quickly decaying and disappearing.' So we still don't have a trustworthy argument to give a man confidence that after we die our soul still exists.

88   'Even if one were to grant your argument more,' he might say, 'and allow not only that our souls existed before we were born, but also that there's nothing to keep some of them from existing after we die and from being reborn and dying again many times—because the soul's nature is so strong that it can endure being born again and again—even if one granted all that but was unwilling to concede further that it doesn't suffer in all of these births and finally perish completely in

b   one of its deaths—and no man,' he would say, 'could know which death and which release from the body would bring the soul its destruction because none of us can detect that—if this is so, then anyone who faces death with confidence is by rights a confident fool, unless he can prove that the soul is absolutely immortal and indestructible. If he cannot, then every time he is about to die he must fear that in its present break with the body his soul may utterly perish.''

c   At this point we all felt rather unpleasant, as we later confessed to each other, because where we had been warmly convinced by the argument, we now seemed thrown back into confusion and doubt—not only about the foregoing discussion, but also about what was yet to be said; we feared we were incompetent judges, and that the subject itself might prove uncertain.

ECHECRATES: By the gods, Phaedo, I sympathize with you completely. Even as I listened to you now, I was moved to

d   say to myself, "Which one shall I believe? How warmly persuasive was Socrates' argument and now how fallen to doubt!" That comparison of our soul to a harmony has always taken an astonishing hold on me, and it did so now. It seemed like a reminder to me that I myself had held that opinion before. Now I need another argument right from the beginning to persuade me that the soul doesn't die with the body. So tell us, for the love of Zeus: How did Socrates run

e   down his rejoinder? Did he show signs of being discouraged, as you say the rest of you were, or did he just calmly come to the argument's rescue? And did his reinforcements suffice?

Tell us everything as accurately as you can.

PHAEDO: Socrates often amazed me, Echecrates, but I had never admired him more. Perhaps having a reply was only to be expected of him, but you had to wonder at the   89
pleasant, respectful, genial way he accepted the young fellows' objections, how perceptively he caught our reaction to them, and how well he cured us and rallied us like defeated, retreating soldiers and got us turned around to follow him and examine the argument with him.

ECHECRATES: How?

PHAEDO: I'll tell you. I was sitting to his right on a little stool next to the cot, and he was much higher than I. He   b
reached down, stroked my head, and squeezed the hair together at the back of my neck—he always teased me about my long hair whenever he got the chance—and said: "Tomorrow, perhaps, you'll cut off this beautiful hair."[15]

"Very likely, Socrates," I said.

"Not if you listen to me, Phaedo."

"Why not?" I asked.

"Because we'll both have to do it today if our argument is dead and we're unable to revive it. If I were you and the   c
answer escaped me, I'd swear an oath like the Argives not to let my hair grow until I'd fought again and defeated these objections of Simmias and Cebes."

"Not even Heracles, they say, could go against two."

"Then call me in as your Iolaus,"[16] he said, "—as long as there's light."

"I will," I said, "not like Heracles, but like Iolaus calling to Heracles."

"It makes no difference, Phaedo. Just be careful we don't catch a certain disease."

"What?" I asked.

"Argument hatred, similar to hatred of people. No   d
affliction is worse, and both strike the same way. People catch hatred of people from trusting a person intensely but without skill and believing the fellow to be absolutely sound and faithful and true, only to discover a little while later that he's

---

[15] **The Greeks** cut their hair as a sign of mourning. "Oath of the Argives" (c, below): Once when the Argives lost some territory to the Spartans, they cut off their hair and vowed not to let it grow again until they had recovered their territory.

[16] **Heracles'** half-brother and trusted companion.

faithless and wicked. They try again and fail. After numerous clashes, especially with people they had considered their closest friends, they finally end up hating everyone and believing that all men are completely corrupt. Haven't you ever seen that happen?"

"Certainly," I said.

"Isn't that shameful, and clear proof that the victim attempts to deal with people without having skill in human affairs? If he had it, he'd believe that things are as they are: that few people are extremely upright or wicked; most are in the middle."

"How do you mean?" I asked.

"Like the extremely large or small. Can you think of anything rarer than finding an extremely large or small man, dog, or anything else? —Or fast or slow, ugly or beautiful, black or white? Haven't you noticed how in everything like that the outer extremes are few and far between, while the ones in the middle are numerous and frequent?"

"Of course," I said.

"If you were holding a depravity contest, don't you think that even there very few would appear exceptional?"

"Most likely," I said.

"Very likely," he replied. "But you led me astray—that's not how men resemble arguments, but like this: When people unskilled in discourse trust an argument as true, only to find a little while later that it seems to them false—whether it actually is or not—and so with another and another—and you know that people who spend their time in disputation especially end up thinking themselves thoroughly wise, unique in perceiving that neither words nor things have anything stable or sound about them but that all reality simply tumbles over and under and never stands still, as though swept along in the Euripus currents."

"That's certainly true," I said.

"Then wouldn't it be a pity, Phaedo, if there were a true, stable argument capable of being understood, and then, after meeting those contradictions that seem now false and now true, a man should blame this inconstancy not on himself or his lack of skill, but on argument, glad in his pain to push the blame from himself onto it, and thus spend the rest of his life hating and reviling argument, deprived of the knowledge and truth about reality?"

"Yes, by Zeus, that would be a pity," I said.

"Then," he said, "let's be careful not to concede to our souls that argument may be unsound; let's say instead that we're not yet sound and must avidly, courageously strive to become so, you and these others for the sake of the rest of your lives, I for the sake of death; because I'm afraid that at present, I regard that very subject not philosophically but tendentiously, like the completely uneducated. They too, when they argue about something, don't care about the truth of the matter; they just want to make their listeners believe that things are as they say. In my present circumstances I think I'll differ from them only in this: I'll be eager to make my views seem true not to my listeners—except incidentally—but to myself. See how selfishly I calculate, my friend: If what I say should really be true, it would be well to believe it. If, however, nothing awaits the dead, I'll at least make this time before my death less unpleasant for you by not lamenting; nor will my folly persist—that would be evil—but soon disappear. In that frame of mind, Simmias and Cebes, I advance on the argument. But you, if you take my advice, will think little of Socrates but much of the truth, and if my ideas seem true you'll agree; if not, resist every argument. And be careful that in my eagerness I don't deceive you as well as myself and then fly off like a bee, leaving my sting behind.

"Well, let's begin. First I'll review your objections, and you remind me of anything I seem to forget. Simmias, I believe, doubts and fears that the soul, though more beautiful and divine than the body, may be a kind of harmony and perish before it. Cebes, I think, agrees with me that the soul is longer-lived, but doubts if anyone can be certain that it doesn't wear out many bodies and, in leaving the last, perish itself, so that this—the soul's destruction—would be death, since the body never stops perishing. Is that what we have to examine, Simmias and Cebes?"

They both agreed that it was.

"First of all," he said "do you reject all the preceding arguments or only some of them?"

"Only some," they said.

"What do you think of the one about learning being recollection, so that our soul must have existed somewhere else before it was imprisoned in the body?"

"I was completely convinced of that at the time," said Cebes, "and I still cling to it like no other argument."

"So do I," said Simmias. "I'll be surprised if I ever change my mind about that."

"You'll have to, my Theban friend," said Socrates, "if you want to stick to your notion that the soul is a harmony, a composite thing composed of the tuned elements of the body. I doubt if you'd even accept that from yourself: that a harmony could be composed before the elements it's composed of exist. Would you?"

"Not at all, Socrates."

"Don't you see that this is what your argument amounts to when you say the soul exists before it comes to human body and form and is composed of elements that don't yet exist? A harmony doesn't resemble what you compared it to because the unharmonized lyre, strings, and notes come into being first, and the harmony is the last thing to be composed and the last to perish. So how does this argument chime with the other?"

"It doesn't," said Simmias.

"But if any argument ought to harmonize, it should be one about harmony."

"It surely should," he said.

"But this one doesn't, so which do you choose: learning as recollection or the soul as a harmony?"

"The first, by far, Socrates. The other just came to me the way it comes to most people—not by demonstration, but by a certain specious probability. I realize that arguments whose demonstrations depend on probability, in geometry or anything else, are imposters that may well deceive us if we don't watch out. But our argument about learning as recollection was demonstrated by means of an assumption worthy of acceptance. We stated, I believe, that our soul existed before it came to a body just as surely as the essence we call 'that which *is*' belongs to the soul. I'm convinced that I've accepted that assumption fully and properly. Therefore, it seems, I may permit neither myself nor another to say that the soul is a harmony."

"Now, Simmias, look at it this way: Do you think it befits a harmony or any other composite to be in a different state than the parts that compose it?"

"Not at all."

"Or to do or to suffer anything other than they?"

"No."

"Then it befits a harmony not to lead but to follow the parts it consists of."

He agreed.

"And it would never sound or vibrate contrary to its own parts, or oppose them in any other way."

"Never."

"Now, isn't it the nature of harmony to be just such a harmony as it was tuned to be?"

"I don't understand," he said.

"Well, suppose it could be tuned more and more fully or less and less fully, if that were possible: Wouldn't it then be more or less of a harmony?"   b

"Of course."

"Is that true of soul? Can one soul be even the slightest bit more or less, or more or less fully, that which it is—soul— than another?"

"No."

"Now consider this, by Zeus: Do we say that one soul has intelligence and excellence and is good, while another has foolishness and depravity and is evil? And is it true to say that?"   c

"It certainly is."

"Then what would a man who posits the soul as a harmony say that excellence and evil in the soul are? Another harmony and a disharmony? And that a good soul, itself a harmony, is in tune and has another harmony in it, while a bad soul is untuned and doesn't have another harmony in it?"

"I don't know," said Simmias. "One who made that assumption would clearly say something like that."

"But we just agreed that no soul is ever more or less of a soul   d than another. That *is* our agreement, isn't it—that no harmony is ever more or less, or more or less fully, a harmony than another?"

"Of course."

"If it's neither more nor less of a harmony, it also harmonizes neither more nor less. Isn't that so?"

"Yes."

"If it harmonizes neither more nor less, does it participate more or less in harmony, or equally?"

"Equally."

"Then since one soul is neither more nor less that which it is—soul—than another, doesn't it harmonize neither more   e nor less?"

"Indeed."

"If that's the case, can one soul participate in more harmony or disharmony than another?"

"No."

Plato

"Then if excellence is harmony and evil disharmony, can one soul participate in more excellence or evil than another?"

"Not a bit."

94   "Actually, Simmias, proper reasoning demands that no soul, if it's a harmony, can participate in any evil. Harmony, being absolutely that—harmony—will never participate in disharmony."

"No."

"Nor soul, being absolutely soul, in evil."

"How could it after what we've said?"

"By this argument, therefore, all souls of all creatures are equally good, if all souls by nature are equally souls."

"I think so, Socrates."

"Do you also think it's a good argument? Would this have
b   happened to it if our assumption were correct—that soul is a harmony?"

"Not at all."

"Now of all the parts of man, can you name one that rules except soul, particularly if it's intelligent?"

"No."

"By opposing or by yielding to bodily states? By pulling to the opposite—not drinking—when heat and thirst arise, for instance, or to not eating when hunger occurs—in these and countless other things don't we see the soul opposing the
c   states of the body?"

"Of course."

"Didn't we agree earlier that if the soul were a harmony, it would never sound contrary to its parts as they get tightened, loosened, plucked, or anything else, but always follow them and never lead?"

"Of course we did," he said.

"Well, haven't we now shown the soul's structure to be the exact opposite of that? It dominates all the parts one might
d   say it consists of, opposes nearly all of them all through life, and masters them in every way, some harshly with painful discipline like gymnastics and medicine, others more gently, admonishing some and threatening others, speaking to desires, passions, and fears like one thing to another. Even Homer presents that, when in the *Odyssey* he says of
e   Odysseus: 'He struck his chest and rebuked his heart:/bear up, old heart, you've endured fouler than this.'[17] Do you

---

[17] The quotation is from *Odyssey* 20.17-18.

think he'd have composed that if he had thought of the soul as a harmony, something led by the states of the body, rather than as something that leads and masters them, far too divine to compare to a hamony?"

"No, I don't think so, Socrates."

"Therefore, my friend, it's wrong for us to call the soul a kind of harmony. We'd be disagreeing both with Homer, it seems—a divine poet—and with ourselves." 95

"That's true," he said.

"Well," said Socrates, "it looks like we've pretty well propitiated Theban Harmony.[18] Now, Cebes, how about Cadmus? What argument shall we propitiate him with?"

"I think you'll find one," said Cebes. "It's amazing how your argument against harmony surpassed my wildest expectations. After hearing Simmias tell what baffled him, I'd have been astounded if anyone could have handled his objection. Then I was astounded when it fell to your argument's very first attack. So I won't be surprised if the same thing happens to Cadmus's objection." b

"Don't talk like that," said Socrates, "you'll jinx our argument and scare it away. Well, we'll leave that to the god, while we Homerically clash with your objection and see if it makes sense. The gist of it is this: You demand that our soul be proved indestructible and immortal. Otherwise any philosopher about to die confident in the belief that he'll fare better over there than if he had lived some other life will be proved a silly but confident fool. Our proof that the soul is a strong, godlike thing that existed before we became men does not indicate its immortality, you say, but only that it's a long-lived thing that existed, knew, and did all sorts of things for an inconceivable length of time before we were born. But it's still not immortal, and by entering a human body it initiated its own destruction, like a disease, because during this life it wears away and finally perishes in what we call death. And, you say, it makes no difference whether it enters a body once or many times. We still must fear every death, because fear becomes anyone but a fool unless he knows and can explain that the soul is immortal. Something like that, I believe, is what you maintain, Cebes. I've purposely repeated it several times so nothing escapes us and so you may add or subtract whatever you'd like." c

[18] **Harmony** was the wife of Cadmus, a legendary king of Thebes (the home town of Cebes and Simmias).

"I've got nothing to add or subtract at the moment," said Cebes. "That's my position."

Socrates sat quietly meditating for some time. "This is no trivial thing you're investigating, Cebes. We'll have to work out the cause of all coming to be and passing away. If you like, I can describe my own experiences in this field, and if I say anything that seems useful to you, you may use it to help settle your doubts."

"Yes, I'd like to hear them," said Cebes.

"All right," he said. "As a young man, Cebes, I had an awesome desire for the wisdom called the investigation of nature. It struck me as a proud thing to know the causes of all things, why each comes to be, passes away, and is. I often agonized over questions like these: 'Are creatures nourished as some people say—when the hot and the cold form a kind of fermentation?[19] What do we think with—our blood? air? fire? Or is it the brain, which produces the sensations of sight, hearing, and smell, from which arise opinion and memory, which in turn, having reached quiescence, give rise to knowledge?' After further exploring the causes of their passing away, as well as what was going on in heaven and earth, I at last concluded that I was eminently unqualified for this kind of study. I'll give you convincing proof of that: These studies so blinded me that I even unlearned things that I—and others too—had once thought I knew clearly, among them the reason why people grow. Before then, I had thought it obvious to everyone that it happened from eating and drinking: that, from food, flesh was added to flesh, bone to bone, and so on for the rest—each substance increased by the addition of its own proper substance, so that a small mass became large and thus a boy grew to a man. That's what I thought—doesn't it seem reasonable to you?"

"Yes," said Cebes.

"Now consider this: When one man or one horse stood next to another and appeared larger, it seemed obvious enough to me that he was larger 'by a head'[20] and still more obvious that ten is more than eight by the addition of two, just as a two-

[19] The various scientific theories mentioned here were current in Socrates' youth.

[20] Part of the confusion in expressions like this arises from the ambiguity of "by," which may denote either *degree of difference* ("taller *by* so much), *manner* or *means* ("we teach *by* precept and

foot ruler is larger than a one-foot ruler because it exceeds it by half its length."

"How does it seem to you now?" asked Cebes.

"Now I'm so far from thinking that I know the cause of any of this that when one is added to one, I can't even tell whether the one that's added becomes two, or the one that's added to, or whether both together become two by the addition of the 97 one to the other. I'm surprised that they were each one when apart and not then two, and became so only after coming together, so that this was the cause of their becoming two— the union formed by placing them next to each other. Nor can I believe that when one is divided in two, this—the division— causes it to become two; because this cause is the opposite of the other. Then two came into being because they were each b brought together and put side by side; now it happens because they're pulled apart and separated from each other. And I no longer believe that I know why one comes to be or for that matter why anything else comes to be, passes away, or is—not by that method. So I've thrown together a way of my own and never take that way any more.

"Once I heard a man reading from a book written, he said, by Anaxagoras, who said mind disposes and causes all things. c That delighted me; it struck me somehow as right that mind should cause everything. If that were true, I thought, then the ordering mind must order all things and put each in its best possible condition. Therefore if one wished to discover the cause of anything's coming to be, passing away, or being, all one had to do was find out why it was best for it to be or to suffer or to do whatever it does. By this account the only thing d a man ought to examine, about himself or anything else, was the best, because then he would also know the worst, since both are objects of the same knowledge.

"So I reasoned, glad because in Anaxagoras I thought that I had found a teacher after my own mind of the causes of all existing things, and that he would first tell me whether the earth is round or flat and then explain the reason and e necessity for this by revealing the best and showing why it was best for the earth to be as it is. Or if he said that it was in the

example," or *agency* or *cause* ("killed *by* the plague"). Confusion results when, as here, one of the former two senses is understood as denoting a cause ("taller *because of* a head").

98 center, why it was best for it to be there. If he'd reveal that, I
was prepared never to long for any other form of cause. And I
was prepared to hear the same for the sun, the moon, and the
other stars, about their relative speeds, revolutions, and other
conditions—how it's best that they do and suffer precisely
what each of them does. I never dreamed, after he said they'd
been ordered by mind, that he'd attribute to them any other

b cause than that it was best for them to be as they are. I assumed
that when he assigned the cause to each one and to all in
common, he'd also explain their common and individual
good. I wouldn't have sold my high hopes for anything, and I
earnestly picked up his books and read them as fast as I could
in order to learn as quickly as possible the best and the worst.

"I was hurled from these towering hopes, my friend, when
I continued reading and saw a man who made no use of mind

c and ascribed no other cause to the ordering of things, but
made causes out of air, ether, water, and all sorts of strange
things. It reminded me of someone who says that Socrates
does all that he does by mind and then attempts to explain the
reasons for each of my actions by saying that I'm sitting here
now, for instance, because my body consists of bones and
sinews; the bones are solid and separated by joints, while the

d sinews can loosen and tighten, and they clothe the bones, as
do the flesh and the skin that hold the bones together. Now,
since the bones swing in their sockets, the sinews, by
contracting and relaxing, presumably enable me to bend my
limbs, and that's why I'm sitting here now all folded up like
this. And he'd give similar causes for my speaking with you—
voice and air and hearing and a thousand more—and neglect

e to mention the true cause: that because the Athenians
resolved it best to condemn me, so I am resolved that it's best
for me to sit here and that it's right to stay and endure
whatever punishment they decree. Otherwise, by the dog, I

99 think these bones and sinews would have been in Megara or
Boeotia long ago, carried there by the resolve that that was the
best, if I hadn't thought it better and more just to submit to
any punishment the city decrees than to run away like a slave.

"To call such things causes is very strange. If one were to
say that without bones and sinews and all the rest I wouldn't
be able to carry out my resolves, that would be true. But to say
that I do what I do because of those things rather than by
deliberately choosing the best—especially when I'm

b supposed to be acting by mind—betrays a lazy, slovenly

manner of speaking. Imagine being unable to distinguish the true cause from something necessary for the cause to exist— which is precisely what most people, groping around in the dark and applying an alien term, seem to call a cause. Therefore one[21] wraps the earth in a vortex so that the sky holds it in place; another shoves air under it for a support, as though it were flat, like a breadboard. No one looks for the c force that now keeps everything in the best possible condition or believes that it has such a superhuman strength. They think they'll discover an Atlas stronger than this one, more immortal and more able to hold all things together. They don't believe that the literally good and the binding holds or binds anything. I'd gladly become a pupil of anyone who could teach me what such a cause is like. But since I was deprived of that, unable to learn it either by myself or from anyone else, would you like me to describe the second-best ship I rigged out to search for the cause, Cebes?"   d

"I certainly would," he said.

"Well, after I'd given up studying the physical world, I thought I'd better be careful and not suffer what observers of solar eclipses do. They ruin their eyes unless they observe the sun's image in water or something. Something like that e occurred to me, and I was afraid I might blind my soul completely by looking at things with my eyes and other senses and trying to grasp them like that. So I decided to take refuge in words and examine the truth of things in them. Perhaps my image doesn't quite fit, because I wouldn't care to admit 100 that you're examining more in images when you observe things in words than when you observe them in actions. At any rate I went at it like this: In each case I take as an assumption the proposition I judge the most valid, and posit as true whatever seems to agree with that—whether it concerns causes or anything else—and as false what does not. But I'll have to make this clearer; I don't think you understand it now."

"Not very well, by Zeus," said Cebes.

"Well, I don't mean anything new—just what I always talk b about and have been talking about all through this discussion. I'm going to try to show you the form of cause I've worked out. I'll go back and start from what I'm always harping on and assume that there is a beautiful itself by itself,

---

[21] **"One . . . another:"** Empedocles and Anaximenes.

and a good itself, a large itself, and everything else itself. If you'll grant me those and agree they exist, I hope to demonstrate causality from them and also discover that soul is immortal."

c   "You've got my agreement," said Cebes, "—go ahead."

"Now see if you also share my opinion of what follows from them. It seems to me that if anything is beautiful besides the beautiful itself, it's beautiful only because it participates in that beautiful itself. And the same for everything else. Do you accept that kind of a cause?"

"Yes," he said.

"I still can't understand those other profound causes. When someone says that a thing is beautiful because of its
d   bright colors or its shape or something, I just get confused. So I let those causes go and stick to my own simple, unskilled, and perhaps silly explanation: that the only thing that makes a thing beautiful is the presence, partnership, or whatever it ought to be called, of the beautiful itself. I won't vouch for the way that it happens, but only for this: that all beautiful things become beautiful by the beautiful. That strikes me as the
e   safest reply to give to myself or anyone else, and as long as I hold on to it, I don't think I'll fall because this answer gives safe footing to me or to anyone else: Beautiful things are beautiful by the beautiful. Do you agree?"

"Yes, I do."

"And large things become large and larger ones larger by largeness; smaller things become smaller by smallness?"

"Yes."

"So you too, I think, would reject the statement that one man is larger than another 'by a head,' and the other smaller
101   by that same thing. You'd insist that one thing is larger than another only by and because of largeness and that the smaller is smaller only by and because of smallness. I think you'd be afraid that if some contradictory argument accosted you and you told it that one man was larger and another smaller 'by a head,' the argument would make you admit first of all that the larger is larger and the smaller smaller by the same thing; secondly, that the larger is larger by 'a head,' which is small—and it would be monstrous for someone to be large
b   because of something small. Wouldn't you be afraid of that?"

Cebes laughed. "I surely would," he said.

"Wouldn't you also be afraid to say that ten is more than eight by two and exceeds it because of that and not because of quantity? Or that a two-foot ruler is larger than a one-foot ruler by its half rather than by largeness? It's all the same fear."

"Certainly," he said.

"And when one is added to one, or divided in two, won't you carefully avoid saying that the addition or the division c caused the two to come about? Won't you loudly exclaim: 'I don't know how anything can come to be except by participating in the peculiar essence of each thing it partakes of. Therefore the only cause I can give for the two coming to be in these cases is participation in duality, in which anything must participate to be two, just as anything must participate in unity to be one.' You'll ignore addings and dividings and all such subtle causes and leave it to wiser men than you to give answers like that, while you, 'scared of your own shadow,' as they say, and of your inexperience, will cling d to the security of our assumption and answer as we have. And if someone sticks to the assumption itself, you'll ignore him and refuse to answer until you've examined its consequences and seen whether they harmonize or not. And when you must explain the assumption itself, you'll do it the same way: You'll take another, higher assumption—whichever one seems best—and keep on until you reach one that's adequate. You won't jumble them all together like the contradictors, e who discuss both the source[22] and its consequences at the same time—not if you want to discover something of reality. Perhaps they don't have any care or explanation for this, but they're so clever they can mix everything up and still please themselves. But you, I think, will proceed as I've said, if you're a philosopher." 102

"That's perfectly true," said Simmias and Cebes together.

ECHECRATES: They were right too, by Zeus. It's amazing, Phaedo, how clear he made that, for anyone with the slightest intelligence.

PHAEDO: Of course, Echecrates. That's how it seemed to all of us at the time.

ECHECRATES: And to all of us hearing it now. But what did they say after that?

PHAEDO: As I recall, after they had agreed with him that each of the forms exists and that all other things get their b

[22] Or "principle." This probably refers to the Good as the governing source of all being. Cf. *Republic* 508 ff.

names from these forms by participating in them, Socrates asked: "If that's the case, then when you say Simmias is larger than Socrates but smaller than Phaedo, aren't you saying that Simmias has both largeness and smallness in him?"

"Yes."

c "Yet you agree that Simmias is not in fact taller than Socrates in the way the words imply. It's not Simmias's nature to be tall because he is Simmias, but because he happens to have largeness. Nor is he taller than Socrates because Socrates is Socrates, but because Socrates has smallness relative to Simmias's largeness."

"True."

"Nor is he shorter than Phaedo because Phaedo is Phaedo, but because Phaedo has largeness relative to Simmias's smallness."

"That's true too."

"Thus Simmias is called both great and small, being in the middle of both. To one person's greatness he submits his
d smallness to be surpassed; to another man's smallness he presents his own surpassing greatness." Socrates smiled. "It sounds like I'm developing a prose style," he said, "but still it's probably much as I say."

Simmias agreed.

"I'm saying this because I want you to share my opinion. It seems to me that largeness itself never consents to be both large and small at the same time, and that even the largeness in us never accepts the small or consents to be surpassed. Either it withdraws and flees when its opposite attacks, or it
e has already perished when smallness arrives—one or the other. It's unwilling to stand up to smallness, accept it, and become other than it was. I can withstand and accept smallness and still be who I am—I'm the same person even if small. But largeness itself doesn't have the nerve to be small while still being large. In the same way, the small in us never consents to become or to be large. No opposite is willing to be
103 or become its opposite while it still is what it was; it either leaves or perishes when that happens to it."

"That seems absolutely true," said Cebes.

Then someone—I forget who—said: "By the gods, didn't we agree earlier to the exact opposite of this—that the larger comes from the smaller and the smaller from the larger, and that all opposites take their becoming from their opposites? It looks to me like we're now saying that this could never happen."

Socrates turned to him and replied: "A brave reminder, but b you don't notice the difference between what we're saying now and what we said then: Then we said that opposite things come from opposite things; now we're saying that the opposite itself will never become opposite to itself—neither the one in us nor the one in nature. Then, my friend, we were discussing things that have these opposites in them and naming them after the opposites; now we're discussing the opposites themselves, which give their names to the things that possess them. Those opposites themselves, we say, will c never consent to accept their becoming from each other." Socrates turned to Cebes: "What he just said didn't confuse you, did it?"

"Not that," said Cebes. "I won't deny, though, that lots of things confuse me."

"So we're agreed on this," said Socrates, "the opposite itself will never be opposite to itself."

"Absolutely," said Cebes.

"Now examine this and see if we agree: Do you say there's a hot and a cold?"

"Yes."

"Are they the same as snow and fire?"

"No, by Zeus." d

"The hot is different from fire, and the cold is different from snow?"

"Yes."

"I think you also agree, as in the previous examples, that snow will never, while remaining what it was, accept the hot and become hot snow. When the hot attacks, snow either withdraws from it or perishes."

"Of course," said Cebes.

"And when cold attacks fire, the fire will either withdraw or perish. It will never, while remaining what it was, dare to accept cold and become cold fire."

"True." e

"With some things, therefore, the situation is this: A form's own name properly designates not only the form itself for all time, but also other things which, though they are not that form, always have its figure[23] whenever they exist. Perhaps

[23] "**Figure**," "shape," and "form" are all synonyms for designating the eternal archetypes. The word translated as "shape" (104b ff.) is *idea*, traditionally transliterated as "idea." This, however, is misleading, since in English "idea" normally refers to something that exists only in the mind. The root of both *eidos* ("form") and *idea* is *id*, "see." Both words denote something seen, the looks or appearance of a thing.

this will make my meaning clearer: The odd, no doubt, must always get the name I just gave it. Isn't that so?"

"Of course."

104 "Only it?—this is my question—or are there some other existing things which, though not identical with the odd, still must always be given that name as well as their own because by their very nature they never abandon the odd? I'm thinking of what happens to three and many other things. But let's look at three. Don't you think that three must always be called odd as well as three, even though the odd is not identical with three? Still, three, five, and half of all the

b numbers have such a nature that each is always odd, though none is identical with the odd; whereas two, four, and the whole other series are always even, although none of them is identical with the even. Do you agree?"

"Certainly."

"Now observe what I'm trying to make clear: Not only do those opposites obviously not accept one another, but all things that have those opposites in them, though not themselves opposed to each other, act as if they refuse to accept the shape that opposes the opposite in them—when it

c attacks they either withdraw or perish. Or shouldn't we say that three will suffer anything and sooner die than become even while still being three?"

"Of course," said Cebes.

"But two surely isn't opposite to three."

"No."

"So it isn't just opposite forms that refuse to accept one another's attack; there are other things too that refuse to accept an opposite's attack."

"True."

"Shall we define, if we can, what kind of things these are?"

"Of course."

d "Well, Cebes, wouldn't they be things that force anything they occupy to possess not only their own shape, but also the shape of something with an opposite?"

"How do you mean?"

"The way we just said. You know that the shape of three compels anything it occupies to be odd as well as three."

"Of course."

"A thing like that, then, would never be attacked by the shape opposite to the figure that makes it odd."

"Of course not."

"And the figure that makes it odd is the odd."

"Yes."

"Whose opposite is the shape of the even."

"Yes."

"Therefore the shape of the even will never invade three." e

"No."

"Then three has nothing to do with the even."

"Nothing at all."

"So three is uneven."

"Yes."

"I said we had to define which things, though they themselves are not opposite to anything, nevertheless refuse to accept an opposite—the way three, though not itself opposite to the even, still refuses to accept the even because it always brings with it the opposite of even, or the way two refuses to accept the odd, fire refuses to accept cold, and so on. So see if you'd agree to this definition: Not only does an 105 opposite refuse to accept its opposite, but anything else that brings with it something opposite to whatever attacks it also refuses to accept the opposite of what it brings with it. Let me remind you again—it doesn't hurt to hear a thing several times: Five will never accept the shape of the even, nor ten, its double, the shape of the odd. This double, to be sure, has its own opposite, but still it will never accept the shape of the odd. Nor will one and a half, or fractions like one-half or one- b third accept the form of the whole. Do you follow and agree, Cebes?"

"Absolutely," he said.

"Then let's take it again from the beginning. And don't answer my questions in the way that I put them, but imitate me—from what we've said, I see another safe way of answering besides that safe way I mentioned at first. If you asked me what must be present in any body to make it warm, I wouldn't give you our safe but stupid answer, 'heat,' but a c more elegant one based on what we've just said: 'fire.' And if you ask what makes a body sick, I won't say disease, but fever. Or if you ask what must be in a number to make it odd, I won't say oddness, but unity, and so forth. Do you understand well enough what I want?"

"Yes, very well," he said.

"All right—what must be present in any body to make it live?"

"Soul," he said.

d   "Is that always true?"

          "How could it be otherwise?"

          "So soul always comes bringing life to whatever it occupies."

          "It surely does."

          "Does life have an opposite?"

          "Yes."

          "What?"

          "Death."

          "Doesn't it follow from what we've agreed on that soul will never accept the opposite of what it brings with it?"

          "Absolutely," said Cebes.

          "What did we just call a thing that never accepts the shape of the even?"

          "Uneven."

          "And things that never accept justice and music?"

e   "Unjust and unmusical."

          "What do we call something that doesn't accept death?"

          "Deathless."

          "Does soul accept death?"

          "No."

          "Then soul is deathless."

          "Indeed."

          "Well, Cebes? Have we proved that soul is immortal?"

          "Very adequately, Socrates."

          "How about this, Cebes: If the uneven were necessarily
106 imperishable, wouldn't three be imperishable too?"

          "Of course."

          "And if the heatless were necessarily imperishable, then whenever heat was applied to snow, wouldn't the snow withdraw safe and unmelted? It surely wouldn't perish or withstand the heat and accept it."

          "True."

          "In the same way, I think, if the coldless were imperishable, then whenever something cold attacked fire, the fire wouldn't perish or go out, but leave and go away safe."

          "Necessarily."

b   "Then mustn't we say the same of the deathless? If the deathless is imperishable, a soul cannot perish when death attacks it. From what we've said, it will never accept death or be dead, any more than three or the odd will ever be even, or fire or its heat ever be cold. 'But,' someone might object, 'even though we agree that the odd never becomes even when the even attacks, what's to prevent the odd from perishing and the even taking its place?' We couldn't argue with him because we haven't agreed that the odd is imperishable. If we had, we could easily argue with him by saying that the odd and three go away when the even attacks. And so for fire and heat and the rest. isn't that true?"

c

"Certainly."

"The same for the deathless: If we agree that the deathless is imperishable, then soul will be imperishable as well as immortal. If not, we'll need another argument."

d

"But that isn't necessary," said Cebes. "Hardly anything could escape destruction if the immortal, which is eternal, accepted destruction."

"And," said Socrates, "I think everyone would agree that god and the very form of life, and whatever else may be deathless, will never be destroyed."

"Not only every man, I think, but also and especially, by Zeus, the gods."

"Then if the deathless is indestructible, mustn't the soul, if it's really deathless, also be indestructible?"

e

"An absolute necessity."

"So when death attacks a man, his mortal part dies, it seems, but his deathless, immortal part withdraws from death and departs, safe and undestroyed."

"Apparently."

"Therefore, Cebes, soul is above all immortal and indestructible, and our souls will exist in Hades."

107

"I've got nothing to say against that, Socrates. I can't doubt our conclusions at all. But if Simmias here or anyone else has an objection, he'd better raise it now because I don't think he can postpone the discussion until some other time."

"Well," said Simmias, "after what we've said I don't have any doubts either. But because of the subject's importance and because of my contempt for human weakness, I'm forced to keep doubting our conclusions."

b

"Well put, Simmias," said Socrates. "You should also examine our original assumptions more carefully, even if they seem trustworthy to you. If you sort them out well enough, I think you'll follow our argument as well as a human being can follow. And once you've made sure of them, you needn't search further."

"True," he said.

"We're right in supposing this much, gentlemen: If the

c

soul is immortal, we must care for it not only for the sake of this time we call life, but for the sake of all time; because if we neglect it, the hazard of death now appears truly appalling. If death were a release from everything, it would be a godsend to the wicked because it would release them from their souls and their evil as well as from their bodies. But now that the soul

d has been proven immortal, it has no refuge or salvation from evil except to become as good and intelligent as it possibly can. The soul brings to Hades nothing but its education and training, which, we are told, greatly help or harm the departed from the very beginning of his journey over there. Each person's own deity, it is said, to whom he was allotted in life, attempts after death to bring him to a certain place where all are gathered and judged, and from where they travel to

e Hades with the guide assigned to lead them from here to there. There they get what they must and stay for as long as they must, until after long cycles of time another guide brings them back here.

"'A single path leads to Hades,' says Aeschylus's
108 Telephus.[24] But I think it's neither single nor one. Otherwise we wouldn't need guides because no one could miss the way on a single path. It must have forks and crossroads, to judge from our rites and sacrifices here.[25] An orderly, intelligent soul follows its guide and doesn't misunderstand the conditions. But a soul that desirously clings to the body, as we

b said earlier, that flutters around it and the visible region for a long time, struggling and suffering, departs reluctantly, forcibly led by the deity assigned to it. And arrived at the place where the others already are, the impure soul that committed impure deeds, joined to foul murder and other atrocities— sister acts of sister souls—why, everyone shuns such a soul, turns his back on it, and refuses to be its guide or journey

c mate; thus it wanders, utterly bewildered, until a certain time has passed, when it gets swept by necessity to its fitting abode. But the soul that lived a pure and moderate life finds guides and journey mates in the gods, and inhabits the place that befits it. For the earth, as I once was persuaded, is such as geographers have never imagined, and filled with astonishing places.''

[24] In a lost tragedy.
[25] Sacrifices to Hecate (a goddess of the dead) were performed on crossroads, which seem to be haunted in all places and times.

"What do you mean, Socrates?" asked Simmias. "I've heard d many things about the earth, but never your belief. I'd like to hear it."

"I don't think it would take the skill of a Glaucus[26] to tell it, Simmias. But to prove it true, I think, would be too hard even for Glaucus's skill. I doubt if I could do it, and even if I had the knowledge, my life now seems too short for so long an argument. But there's nothing to stop me from telling what I believe the earth's shape is like and the places it has." e

"That will do," said Simmias.

"Well, first of all," said Socrates, "if the earth is a sphere in the middle of heaven, I believe it needs neither air nor any other such force to keep it from falling. Its own equilibrium 109 and the sky's complete similarity to itself are sufficient to hold it in place. A balanced thing placed in the center of a uniform thing will, being self-similar, have no tendency to move, but remain stationary. That, then, is my first conviction."

"A correct one too," said Simmias.

"Secondly, I believe, the earth is huge, and we who live between the Phasis River and the Pillars of Heracles[27] inhabit b only a tiny portion of it, settled around the sea like ants or frogs around a swamp. And many other peoples inhabit many similar places because the earth is completely covered with hollows, diverse both in shape and in size, into which flow water, mist, and air. The earth itself, however, is pure and rests where the stars are: in the pure heaven, which most authorities call ether. Air, mist, and water are the ether's c sediment and settle in the hollows of the earth. We, inhabiting the hollows, fail to perceive the earth's true situation and imagine ourselves living on top, just as people living on the ocean floor would suppose themselves living on top of the sea; and viewing the sun and the other stars through the water, they would believe that the sea was the sky because their weakness and torpor would prevent them from reaching d the surface and stretching up to see how much fairer and

---

[26] It is uncertain which Glaucus is intended. Perhaps Glaucus of Samos, who was credited with the invention of welding.

[27] The traditional boundaries of the civilized world for the Greeks. The Phasis flows into the east side of the Black Sea near Poti; the Pillars of Heracles are the Straits of Gibralter. The "sea" is the Mediterranean.

purer our region is than their own, or from ever hearing about it from someone else who had seen it.

"The same thing happens to us. We live in a hollow of the earth and think we live above, and we call the air heaven, as though the stars moved through it. This is the same situation because our weakness and torpor prevent us from going up to the surface of the air. If a man could grow wings and fly to the top, he could stretch up and see, like a fish leaping out of the water to view the things here, the things over there; and he would know, if his nature were strong enough to endure the sight, that that was the true sky and the light and the earth. This earth, the stones here, and our entire region have been corrupted and eaten away, as in the sea things get eaten by brine; nothing worth mentioning grows; and wherever there's earth you find nothing but caves, sand, slime, and implacable mud, which are nothing compared to our beauties here. But the contrast between the things up there and the ones down here would appear even greater. If I may tell you a story, Simmias, it should be worth hearing what it's really like up there on the earth under the sky."

"We'd enjoy hearing it, Socrates."

"Well, my companion, if you contemplate the earth itself from above, they say it looks like one of those balls made of twelve different-colored patches of leather, and its colors make the colors that painters use here look like samples. There the whole earth consists of such colors, much purer and brighter than ours. One patch is an amazingly beautiful purple, another yellow, another whiter than chalk or snow, and so on for more numerous and beautiful colors than we've ever seen. Even these hollows, filled with air and water, present a form of color as they glisten amid the other colors, so that the earth's form appears as one continuous, mottled pattern.

"Such is the earth, they say, and on it grow plants of analogous beauty: trees, fruits, and flowers. It likewise has mountains, and rocks correspondingly beautiful in their clarity, smoothness, and color, of which our precious stones, such as cornelians, jaspers, and emeralds, are but lovely fragments. There they all are like that, but even more beautiful, because those rocks are pure, not corrupted and eaten away like ours by rot, salt, and those elements that settle down here and infect our rocks and our earth and all plants and animals here with ugliness and disease. The true earth is adorned with all those ornaments and with silver and gold and similar beauties, which lie naturally exposed because they're many and large and completely cover the earth, which makes it one of the happiest sights.

111

"And many animals, including men, live up there, some of them inland, some around the air as we around the sea, others on islands lying close to the mainland and washed by the air. In a word, what water and the sea are to us for our use, the air is to them for theirs, and what air is to us, ether is to them. Their climate is so temperate that they live free from disease and much longer than we, and they excel us in seeing, hearing, thinking, and everything else by as much as air is purer than water and ether purer than air. And they have sacred groves and temples which are truly inhabited by gods, whose voices and prophecies they hear and whom they perceive and commune with directly. The sun and the moon and the stars appear to them as they are, and everything else coincides to make their happiness complete.

b

c

"Such is the nature of both the earth as a whole and its features. And numerous regions, they say, occupy the hollows all around the earth; some deeper and wider than the one in which we live, some with a deeper and narrower gorge than ours, others shallower and broader. These gorges penetrate the earth and connect with each other by wider or narrower passages, and they have outlets through which they pour much water out of and into each other like bowls. And gigantic, ever-flowing rivers of hot and cold waters flow under the ground. There is also much fire and great rivers of fire, and many rivers of mud, some clearer and some more turbid, as in Sicily rivers of mud flow before the lava, and then the lava itself.

d

e

"These substances flow around to the various regions and flood them, moving up and down like a seesaw inside the earth. The seesaw's nature is something like this: One of the earth's chasms is otherwise the largest and penetrates the entire earth. This is the one Homer refers to when he says, 'Far below, where the abyss lies deepest under the ground.'[28] Elsewhere he and many other poets call this abyss 'Tartarus.' All the rivers flow into and out of that chasm, each becoming like the earth that it flows through. They all flow in and out of there because the liquid has no foundation or bottom.

112

b

[28] The quotation is from *Iliad* 8.14.

Therefore it seesaws up and down in continual waves, and the air and the wind around it do the same, following the liquid as it rushes now to the earth's far side and now to its near; and as in breathing we inhale and exhale a constant flow of air, so there the air undulates with the liquid and creates terrific blasts as it moves in and out.

c   "When the water recedes to the region called 'down,' they say, the streams flow into the places on the far side of the earth, filling them as if pumped. And when it leaves there and surges back here, it fills these streams again, which swell and flow through their channels and through the earth and reach the places to which they've been led: seas, lakes, rivers, and

d   springs. After traversing, some of them numerous regions in an extensive circuit, others fewer places in a more limited round, they again enter the earth and fall back into Tartarus, some at a point much lower than where they came out, others only a little lower. But all flow in lower than they flowed out, many on the side opposite their outlets, many on the same side. Some go completely around in a circle, once or several times, spiraling in the earth like snakes until they've dropped

e   as low as they can and fall back into Tartarus. They can descend from either side as far as the center, but no farther, because either side of center lies uphill to both sets of streams.

        "There are many large and multifarious streams, but four of these many, they say, are the largest. The largest of these flows in a circle farthest from the center and is called Ocean. Directly opposite it and flowing in the opposite direction is the Acheron,[29] which traverses other desolate regions and

113   then dips underground to reach the Acherusian lake, where the souls of most of the dead arrive and remain for certain ordained times—some shorter, some longer—before being sent out to be born again as living creatures. The third river, emerging between those two, falls near its mouth into a large place burning with fire, and forms a lake bigger than our sea, boiling with water and mud. From there it recedes in a circle,

b   turbid and muddy, and coils around in the earth, touching numerous places, including the shores of the Acherusian lake; but it does not mingle its waters. After winding several times under the ground, it issues at a lower point of Tartarus. This river is called Pyriphlegethon,[30] and lava streams spout

[29] "Woe."
[30] "Flame."

up fragments of it wherever they appear on the earth. The fourth river bursts out opposite to Pyriphlegethon and empties into a wild and terrible place, they say, all blue-gray, like lapis lazuli. They call this the Stygian river, and the lake   c
that it forms the Styx.[31] After falling into the lake this river picks up terrible force, dives back into the earth, coils contrary to Pyriphlegethon, and meets it head on in the Acherusian lake. It also mingles with no other water, and it too circles around, then plunges into Tartarus opposite to Pyriphlegethon. The name of this fourth river, say the poets, is Cocytus.[32]

"Such is the nature of those regions, and when the dead   d
arrive at the place to which each one's guiding deity brings him, they are first judged for the piety and beauty of their lives. And those found to have lived unexceptional lives proceed to the Acheron, board certain boats that await them, and cross to the lake where they live until they're purified and absolved, suffering punishment for any crimes they committed and winning honors for their good deeds, each according to his merits. But those judged incurable by the   e
enormity of their crimes—great and frequent sacrilege, lawless murders, and other transgressions—a fitting dispensation hurls them into Tartarus, whence they never return.

"Those, on the other hand, found to have committed great but curable crimes—violence against parents, for instance,   114
perpetrated in anger and bringing lifelong remorse, or murders committed in passion—those too are necessarily plunged into Tartarus, where they remain for a year until a wave washes them out, the murderers to Cocytus and wailing, the parricides to Pyriphlegethon and flame. And when the rivers carry them to the Acherusian lake, they shout and cry out to the ones they killed or assaulted, imploring and beseeching them to let them step out and be taken into the   b
lake. And if they persuade them, they emerge and cease from their suffering; if not, they're again swept back into Tartarus and back to the rivers, and they find no rest from this torment until they persuade their victims. For this is the penalty imposed upon them by the judges.

"Those judged, however, to have led lives distinctively

---

[31] "Hate."
[32] "Wailing."

c pious are freed from these underground regions, released from them as from jail, and ascend to pure habitations where they live on the earth. And the ones sufficiently purified in philosophy live entirely without bodies for all future time and go to homes even more splendid than those, which would be hard to describe even if my time should suffice. But for the sake of what we've already described, Simmias, we must do all in our power to partake of knowledge and excellence in this life. For the prize is beautiful, and great is the hope.

d "To insist that these things are just as I have described them would not be the act of a sensible man. But to believe either this or something much like it concerning our souls and their dwellings—since the soul has been proven immortal—that seems to me to be a fitting belief and one worth taking a chance on—because the risk is beautiful—and we must sing these things to ourselves like incantations, which is why I've drawn the tale out to such length.

"That, then, is why a man must have confidence for his
e soul—whoever in this life has spurned the pleasures of the body and its adornment as alien things that do more harm than good and has pursued instead the pleasures of learning, adorning his soul with ornaments not alien, but proper to
115 it—temperance, justice, courage, freedom, and truth—and so awaits the journey to Hades. You, Simmias and Cebes and the rest of you," he said, "will each make this journey at some later time. But now 'my appointed hour calls,' as a tragic hero might say, and it's nearly time for my bath. I think it best to bathe before drinking the poison to spare the women the trouble of washing a corpse."

b When he had finished, Crito spoke: "Well, Socrates. Now, do you have some request to make of me or these others about your sons or anything else? What can we do that would especially please you?"

"Nothing new, Crito," he replied. "Just what I've always said: If you care for yourselves you'll please me and mine and yourselves whatever you do, even if you don't promise it now. But if you neglect your own selves and refuse to live following the trail of our present discussion and of our earlier ones, you'll accomplish nothing, no matter how many fervent
c promises you make at the moment."

"We'll be eager to do as you say," said Crito. "But how shall we bury you?"

"However you like," he said, "—if you can catch me and I

don't slip away from you." He chuckled quietly, then looked at us and said: "Gentlemen, I can't persuade Crito that I am the Socrates who is talking with you and marshaling these arguments. He thinks I am that body he'll soon see as a corpse, and he asks how he should bury me. That long speech   d
I just made—how after drinking the poison I'll no longer be with you but leave to enjoy certain happinesses enjoyed by the blessed—seems to have been wasted on him, though I made it to console both you and myself. Therefore I want you to give Crito the opposite security that he gave the jury: He swore to them that I would stay here; now you swear to him that after I die I won't stay here but depart, so that he'll take it   e
more lightly and not grieve for my sake when he sees me being cremated or buried, as though I were suffering something terrible, or say at my funeral that he is laying out Socrates or following or burying me. You must understand, my excellent Crito, that speaking falsely is not only an error in itself; it also puts evil in our souls. So you must be of good cheer and say it's my body you're burying and bury it however you think best and most customary."   116

With that he got up and went into another room to bathe. Crito followed him and told us to wait. So we waited, discussing and going back over what had been said, and sometimes dwelling on the great misfortune that had befallen us; we felt we would live like orphans deprived of their father for the rest of our lives. After he had bathed and his children had been brought to him—he had two little sons and a big   b
one—and the family women had come in and he had talked with them in the presence of Crito and made his requests, he told them to leave and came back to us. He had spent a long time inside, and it was now close to sunset. He returned clean from the bath and sat down, and little was said after that. A servant of the Eleven came in and went over to him. "Socrates," he said, "I know I won't have to blame you like   c
the others for getting angry and cursing me when I have to inform them from the officials that it's time for the poison. Since you've been here, I've found you to be the noblest, gentlest, best man we've ever had in here, and I know you're not angry with me but with those you realize are responsible. And now—you know what I've come for. Goodbye; try to bear this necessity as lightly as you can." He burst into tears,   d
turned, and started to leave.

Socrates looked after him. "I'll do that," he said, "and

goodbye to you." Then he turned back to us. "What an excellent man!" he said. "All the while I've been here, he would come in and see me, talk with me sometimes, and was always the most civil of men; and now how nobly he weeps for me. But come, Crito, let's do as he says. Have them bring the poison if it's ground. If it's not, tell the man to grind it."

e "But Socrates," said Crito, "I think the sun is still on the mountains and hasn't gone down yet. Anyway, I know of others who've put it off for a long time after it was announced, eating and drinking merrily and even sleeping with the ones they love. So don't hurry. There's still time."

"It's reasonable for them to do that, Crito," said Socrates, "—they think they profit by it. It's also reasonable for me not
117 to do it, because I think a short delay will bring me no other profit than contempt in my own eyes for clutching at life and being thrifty when there's nothing to save. So please do as I say, Crito."

Crito nodded to the slave standing near him. The boy went out, and after a long wait he came back with the poisoner, who was carrying a cup full of poison. Socrates looked at the fellow and said: "You understand these things, my good man. What must I do?"

"Just drink the poison and walk around until your legs feel
b heavy, and then lie down. The rest will take care of itself." He handed him the cup.

Socrates took it, Echecrates, and calmly, without trembling or turning pale or changing his expression, but simply staring in his usual wide-eyed way, he asked the man: "What about pouring a libation from this? May I?"

"We only ground as much as we thought you should drink, Socrates."

c "I see," he said. "Still, I suppose one may—even must— pray to the gods that the move from here to there be a fortunate one. That's what I pray for; may it be granted." And raising the cup he lightly and cheerfully drained it. Until then most of us had held back our tears pretty well, but when we saw him drink, we no longer could do so. I was so overcome that I burst into tears, buried my face in my cloak, and wept for myself—not for him, but for my own misfortune
d at losing a companion like him. Crito had already got up and moved away when he found he could no longer keep back his tears, and Apollodorus, who had been crying all along, now burst into such loud weeping and complaining that no one

could keep from breaking down except Socrates himself.

"Gentlemen," he said, "you surprise me. That's why I sent the women away—to avoid jarring scenes like this because I've heard that one ought to die in peace. So control yourselves and keep quiet."   e

We were ashamed and restrained ourselves. Socrates walked around until he said his legs felt heavy, then lay down on his back as he had been told. The man who had given him the poison felt his feet and legs from time to time to test them, and finally he pinched his foot hard and asked if he felt it. Socrates said no. Next he squeezed his calves, and so on up his legs, showing us how they were setting and growing cold, and he said when it reached his heart he'd be gone.   118

When the cold had spread about to his waist, Socrates uncovered his head—he had covered it earlier—and spoke for the last time: "Crito," he said, "we owe Asclepius a rooster. Please see that he gets it."[33]

"I will," said Crito. "Do you have anything else to say?"

But there was no reply, and a little while later he shuddered and then lay still. The man uncovered him, and his eyes were set. Crito closed his mouth and his eyes.

That was the end of our companion, Echecrates, a man who in our experience was the best, the wisest, and the most just of his time.

---

[33] **Asclepius** was the god of healing. It was customary to sacrifice a rooster to him after recovering from a serious illness, which in Socrates' case must be life.

bibliography

Only a few of the many books about Plato and his works can be given here. For a full bibliography the reader may consult Guthrie's *History* (listed below). The beginner may want to start by reading a general article on Plato, such as "Plato and the Academy" in *A History of Greek Literature* by Albin Lesky (New York, 1966), pp. 505-547, or "Plato" by Gilbert Ryle in *The Encyclopedia of Philosophy*, edited by Paul Edwards (New York, 1967), Vol. VI, pp. 314-333. Many of the books listed below have chapters devoted to the historical background of Plato's times; for a fuller treatment see *Plato and his Contemporaries: A Study in Fourth-Century Life and Thought* by G.C. Field (London, 1930).

Allen, R.E., ed., *Studies in Plato's Metaphysics* (London, 1965). A collection of essays.

Anton, J.P., and Kustas, G.L., eds., *Essays in Ancient Greek Philosophy* (Albany, N.Y., 1971).

Bambrough, Renford, ed., *New Essays on Plato and Aristotle* (London, 1965).

Bluck, R.S., *Plato's Phaedo* (London, 1955).

Copleston, Frederich C., *A History of Philosophy*, Vol. I, Part I (New York, 1962).

Cornford, Francis, M., *Before and After Socrates* (Cambridge, 1932).

———, "The Doctrine of Eros in Plato's Symposium," in *The Unwritten Philosophy* (Cambridge, 1950).

Dover, K.J., *Greek Homosexuality* (Cambridge, Mass., 1978).

Friedländer, Paul, *Plato*, Vol. I, *An Introduction* (2nd ed., Princeton, 1969).

Gould, Thomas, *Platonic Love* (London, 1963).

Grube, G.M.A., *Plato's Thought* (London, 1935).

Gulley, Norman, *Plato's Theory of Knowledge* (London, 1963).

Guthrie, W.K.C., *A History of Greek Philosophy*, Vol. IV, *Plato, The Earlier Period* (Cambridge, 1975). Extensive bibliography.

Jaeger, Werner, *Paedeia: The Ideals of Greek Culture*, Vol. II, *In Search of the Divine Centre* (Oxford, 1943).

Patterson, Robert L., *Plato on Immortality* (University Park, Pa., 1965).

Randall, J.H., Jr., *Plato, Dramatist of the Life of Reason* (New York, 1970).

Rosen, Stanley, *Plato's Symposium* (New Haven, 1968). Extensive bibliography.

Shorey, Paul, *What Plato Said* (Chicago, 1933).

Solmsen, Friedrich, *Plato's Theology* (Itaca, N.Y., 1942).

Taylor, A.E., *Plato, The Man and His Work* (London, 1926). A standard work.

_____, *Plato* (London, 1922: Ann Arbor Paperback reprint, *The Mind of Plato*, 1960).

Vlastos, Gregory, ed., *The Philosophy of Socrates* (Doubleday Anchor Books, 1971). A collection of essays.

_____, *Plato*, Vol. I, *Metaphysics and Epistemology*, Vol. II, *Ethics, Politics, and Philosophy of Art and Religion* (Doubleday Anchor Books, 1971). Collections of essays.

White, Nicholas, P., *Plato on Knowledge and Reality* (Indianapolis, 1976).